Clarence Darrow

CLARENCE DARROW

Miriam Gurko

Thomas Y. Crowell Company · New York

Copyright © 1965 by Miriam Gurko
All rights reserved. No part of this book may
be reproduced in any form, except by a reviewer,
without the permission of the publisher.
Designed by Albert Burkhardt
Manufactured in the United States of America
by the Vail-Ballou Press, Inc., Binghamton, New York
Library of Congress Catalog Card No. 65-13138
First Printing

This one is for Leo

Foreword

Clarence Darrow was one of America's greatest lawyers, but the more successful he was in the courtroom, the more he longed to devote himself to writing. For years he cherished the dream of retiring from law and becoming an author. Whenever he could take time off from his practice or his political activities, he turned to literary creation. Although his writing had to take second place to a legal career that encompassed about two thousand cases, including some of the most difficult and most controversial trials of the period, Darrow managed to produce a surprising number of stories, articles, pamphlets, and books. His subjects covered literary criticism, philosophy, religion, economics, labor problems, criminology, capital punishment, prohibition, and divorce. In addition to nonfiction, he turned out two novels and many short stories.

He also lectured and debated throughout his life on the same wide range of topics. Many of these talks were later published. Even his legal speeches, particularly his famous jury addresses, were often as "literary" and as revealing of their author as were the works written specifically for publication. Many of the legal pieces were printed as separate pamphlets.

All these items provide a rich collection of material for Darrow's biographers. A listing of my principal sources must therefore begin with Darrow's own writings, especially his autobiography, *The Story of My Life*. I wish to thank Charles Scribner's Sons for permission to quote from it. *Farmington*, the slightly fictionalized account of Darrow's boyhood, supplied descriptions of his earliest years in Ohio and of his parents.

A large part of Darrow's work appeared in scattered articles or pamphlets, now for the most part out of print and difficult to obtain. Fortunately, his most important trial summations and legal addresses were assembled a few years ago by Arthur Weinberg in *Attorney for the Damned*. What William Dean Howells said of one of Darrow's court speeches can be applied to this entire volume: "As interesting as a novel." An equally valuable selection of Darrow's nonlegal writings is contained in *Verdicts Out of Court*, edited by Arthur and Lila Weinberg. Both these books contributed greatly to my own. My deep appreciation goes to Mr. and Mrs. Weinberg for their kind and helpful reception when I was doing research in Chicago.

One of the chief sources for Darrow's political activities was *Altgeld's America* by Ray Ginger. Another of Mr. Ginger's books, *Six Days or Forever?* provided a good deal of information on the Scopes trial in Dayton. Material for this same trial and for the Sweet case came from *Let Freedom Ring* by Arthur Garfield Hays, who was associated with Darrow on both occasions. The labor trials and their backgrounds were based on a variety of sources, but the single work giving the most pertinent account of this subject was *Dynamite* by Louis Adamic.

The two biographies, *Clarence Darrow* by Charles Yale Harrison and *Clarence Darrow for the Defense* by Irving Stone, were also useful, and the little hand-printed tribute by Allen Crandall, *The Man from Kinsman,* provided illuminating sidelights. Mr. Stone's book, in particular, contained many details about Darrow's private life, gleaned from interviews and correspondence with friends, relatives, and associates. The quoted comments of Jessie and Ruby Darrow and Darrow's reply to Ruby came from this source. The remarks exchanged between Darrow and Earl Rogers are from *Final Verdict* by Adela Rogers St. Johns. Other important sources, too numerous to mention here, are listed in the bibliography.

Thanks are due to the Newberry Library, the Library of the University of Chicago, and the Chicago Public Library for permitting me to examine manuscripts, letters, and other items in their collections, and to the librarians of these institutions and of the New York Public Library for their patient and generous assistance.

Contents

Clarence Darrow

1

Amirus Darrow

Amirus Darrow felt he could not, in good faith, serve as a minister. He had just graduated from the Meadville Theological Seminary and had been offered a parish by the Unitarian Church. On the face of it, his way seemed clear and filled with promise. When he had received his first degree from Allegheny College in Meadville, Pennsylvania, his belief in religion was so strong that he had gone directly into the Unitarian seminary, fully prepared to spend his life in the serene paths of the ministry.

It seemed the ideal profession for a man of his temperament. He was quiet, scholarly, reflective, with an overwhelming love for books. His son Clarence was to call him a visionary and dreamer, yet deeply sympathetic and responsive to people, passionately concerned with justice and tolerance.

But during his years in the seminary, he began to ask questions which neither his teachers nor the theological works he studied could answer. By the time he graduated his faith had been replaced by doubt. Far from being disturbed by his loss of faith, he decided that doubt was the beginning of wisdom. It was not enough merely to absorb knowledge. One must question as well.

Rejecting the offer of a parish, he put aside the well-defined, secure life of a minister and set off on a voyage of intellectual exploration. He had no money and no means of earning a living. He was going against the ways of the conventionally religious small towns in which he would live. All this required a formidable degree of courage and dedication. It was to be a voyage filled with hardships that never became easier, but which Amirus would never think of abandoning. Life to him was an unremitting search for truth and knowledge, and nothing else mattered. Nothing else really existed.

Where does the life of a man begin? At what point does he acquire the unique personality, the particular viewpoints that set him off from others? How much of what he becomes is the result of his family background or the place in which he lives or the historical period into which he is born? The life of Clarence Darrow, that amazing composite of skepticism and human sympathy, that tireless defender of unpopular causes, began, in a sense, when Amirus Darrow deliberately turned his back on the well-grooved life of a minister and set off on the rocky path of the dissenter.

Amirus was not alone on this path. When he was very young, still a student at Ellsworth Academy in Amboy, Ohio, he had been drawn to another student, Emily Eddy, whose interest in books and ideas was as great as his own. Their backgrounds were very similar. Both were the children of farmers and each was the only child in the family with any interest in books; they were able to provide for each other a response lacking in their own homes. Both came from families whose strong belief in individual freedom had led them to maintain stations on the Underground Railway for escaped slaves before the Civil War. Both families had come from Connecticut to Ohio when it was still practically frontier country.

The first Darrow had left England for America about 1680, together with fifteen other men, all bearing a grant from the king of England for the town of New London, Connecticut. Clarence Darrow, in disclaiming any credit for coming from an old family, once wrote that many people said the Darrows' pedigree was so old that the family ran back as far as Adam and Eve, though he himself would not guarantee the title.

Amirus and Emily were married shortly before he entered Allegheny College. They had little money. In addition to attending school, Amirus had to work at whatever odd jobs he could find. But the rigors of living as poor students were only a preamble to the difficulties that faced them after Amirus deliberately rejected the security of a minister's life. He was untrained for any other kind of work; the young couple had no money saved, no financial resources, no prospects whatever. He tried several kinds of work, ending with carpentry. This seemed less unsatisfactory than anything else, so he set himself up as a maker of wooden furniture.

In the meantime they had moved from Meadville to the rural village of Kinsman in the northeast corner of Ohio. Amirus made chairs, tables, and beds for the local farmers and townspeople. As a sideline he also became the town undertaker, using a hearse that doubled as a delivery truck for the furniture.

Children arrived at intervals of about two years until there were eight—of whom one died in infancy—although they certainly, said Clarence later, "could not afford so many doubtful luxuries." Their fifth child, Clarence, was born on April 18, 1857.

Several years later the Darrows bought the house which became their permanent home. It was an odd, octagonal building, with a large yard in which they raised chickens and kept a cow and horses. Just behind the house was Amirus' workshop.

Kinsman was a quiet little Midwest village of about four or five hundred people. Small white wooden houses lined the tree-shaded streets or stood close to the banks of a winding river. Beyond the town itself were woods and gently rolling fields, interlaced with streams.

It was an almost idyllically peaceful town, but it was not the place for a man like Amirus. The valley in which the town lay was very narrow, and so too, wrote Clarence, were the people who lived there. They were chiefly farmers— Ohio, like most of the United States at that time, was still agricultural—with some shopkeepers and small artisans.

They knew little of the outside world, even less of the world of books and ideas that to Amirus constituted the real world. If anything, they regarded book learning with suspicion. They held orthodox political and social views and were devout churchgoers, accepting the tenets of their faith unquestioningly. They felt that pleasure was sinful, cities were evil, and that countrymen, especially farmers, were the salt of the earth. Their fixed political ideas were held almost as part of divine revelation.

To these people Amirus Darrow was "the village infidel," the freethinker who read the blaspheming works of Voltaire and Tom Paine. He was the heretic, the man who always took the opposing view in any discussion. On almost all religious and social questions he stood alone. For all its peace and loveliness, Kinsman was a place of exile and isolation for his spirit.

One of the burning issues of the day on which Amirus could be found arguing with his neighbors was the question of slavery. As a border state, Ohio was divided in its views, sometimes quite bitterly. Amirus, with his intense belief in individual freedom and human dignity, was a zealous abolitionist, feeling that the slaves must be freed at any cost. One of the abolitionist leaders who inspired his respect was William Henry Seward. When Amirus was summoned from the debate he was carrying on in the tinsmith's shop across the street to see his newborn son, he announced that the boy would be called Seward. Emily, however, insisted on the name Clarence but agreed to Seward as the baby's middle name. Clarence himself was never happy with his first name. His only consolation was to be that his friends could never coin any nickname "half so inane" as his real one.

Thus Clarence Seward Darrow was launched, on the rising tide of the Civil War.

Perhaps the greatest difference between Amirus and his neighbors was his passion for books. One of Clarence's earliest memories was of the books that filled every corner of the house. The family was large, wrote Clarence, the house was small, but there were books everywhere, hundreds and hundreds of them. They were crammed into shelves, piled on tables and chairs, heaped on the floor. There was barely enough money for basic necessities, yet somehow books were bought, books in Latin and Greek and Hebrew, books on history and law and social theory and literature. Amirus read late into every night. Long after going to bed, Clarence would wake and see the light still shining under the door which separated his room from his father's study. During the day, no matter how busy he was or how urgent the immediate job, Amirus would spend an hour or two reading. He lived for his books and for the pure pursuit of knowledge, going through his daily work "in a walking trance." No one in the whole region, said Clarence, knew so much of books and so little of life. The wonders of the world were contained for him largely between the covers of a book.

Like her husband, Emily Darrow also had a profound respect for books and knowledge, and spent far more time reading than the other women in the area. She was well informed on current issues and an ardent follower of the woman's-rights movement which was at that time beginning to stir. She was as deeply concerned as Amirus with the humanitarian and liberal causes of the period. She was, for her day, an "advanced woman." This was still a rare phenomenon, and she found little response or companionship among the Kinsman housewives.

Emily was also an energetic and practical woman. She was as efficient as Amirus was visionary. Where he dreamed of the ideal world, she pitched into the real world with intelligence and courage. It was her good management and firm, controlling will that kept the family going. She worked endlessly, keeping them all fed and clothed and the house in order, and at the same time contrived to give Amirus breathing space for his beloved studies. She saw to it that her children received a better than average education, despite their meager finances. It was her hand and brain, wrote Clarence, that provided the guiding force in the practical affairs of life.

She was not demonstrative or openly affectionate. Nor for that matter was Amirus, though he had perhaps the gentler nature of the two. They were New Englanders not only by descent but by tradition and temperament as well. Open expressions of love would have been considered signs of weakness. Clarence never remembered either of his parents kissing their children or holding them in their arms. They were essentially kind and just, and performed heroic feats of self-denial for the sake of their family. But, to Clarence's later regret, they never established any feeling of companionship or closeness with their children. They studied with them, but never played with them. There was nothing approaching an easygoing atmosphere of gaiety and warmth. The prevailing atmosphere was one of restraint and serious dedication to study.

The brothers and sisters often quarreled. They had a strong family feeling and helped each other unreservedly in times of crisis, but when they wanted companionship and affection they went outside their home. They may have loved each other dearly, wrote Clarence, but they were too proud and well trained to say anything about it.

If they were not encouraged to express their love for each other, however, they were taught to love humanity as a whole, especially that part of it which was oppressed. Amirus and Emily supported the many humanitarian and Utopian movements which flourished during that period. They were especially involved in the cause of the Negro. Abolitionists, traveling through the countryside trying to rouse people against slavery, held their meetings in the Darrow shop or stayed over at the Darrow home. The Darrows helped the Underground Railway in getting escaped slaves to the North. Clarence was sometimes put on the top of a wagonload in which a concealed slave was being smuggled to the next station on his way to freedom.

Emily Darrow died at the age of forty-four, when Clarence was fourteen. His grief and despair made him realize how much love there had been after all, though it was never spoken of. Her "infinite kindness and sympathy," he wrote later, had done much to shape his life.

It was now Amirus, with his combination of learning, skepticism, and gentleness, who continued to set the pattern for Clarence's own personality. Amirus taught his children never to accept, always to question. His feeling of almost personal responsibility for the unfortunates of the earth, his determination to think and act independently no matter how much it went against the social, political, or religious grain of his surroundings, were to be reflected again and again in the course of his son's life. Knowing Amirus, one finds it easier to understand Clarence.

2

Ohio Schoolboy

When Clarence was six, he entered the district school. His education had started much earlier, however. Amirus, with his conviction that learning was the great if not the only key to life, began teaching his children almost as soon as they were old enough to play with the colored alphabet blocks strewn around the house. It seemed to Clarence that he had always known how to read. He must have learned at a very early age, but it was not young enough to suit Amirus, who held up the example of the oldest son, Everett, who had learned still earlier. Worse than this, there was the awful example of John Stuart Mill, the English philosopher and economist, who began studying Greek at the age of three. Amirus saw no reason why his own children could not do as well and told them so over and over. Clarence, who infinitely preferred play to study, hated to hear about John Stuart Mill and loathed John Stuart Mill's father who not only had made his own son's life miserable (Clarence was sure), but caused grief to thousands of other little boys whose fathers expected the same of them.

Amirus took his children's education seriously. He was always calling them from their games, to Clarence's distress, in order to teach them or hear their school lessons. Every night, as they sat around the kerosene lamp, he supervised their studies, supplementing what they learned in school. His great ambition was to give his children the education which would help them escape into the wide world beyond the narrow valley. As Clarence grew older, he realized the tragedy of his father's life: the scholar forced to live as an obscure woodworker, the bitter contest waged against the prejudices and conventions of the little town.

Clarence himself took a dim view of formal education. He felt that most of his studies at school were a waste of time and that teachers were the natural enemies of small boys. He felt that very little of what he was taught had any connection with actual life. In those days learning was entirely by rote; children were not encouraged to think for themselves. He complained later that his early education had consisted mainly of memorizing arbitrary rules and generally useless facts. Children were taught not how to think but what to think, and the "what" was determined by local beliefs and customs. Any teacher departing from the established "truths" was soon dismissed.

Clarence had great difficulty with grammar. No matter how hard he struggled, egged on by Amirus and his teachers, the parts of speech, especially the verb, remained a veiled mystery to him. His teachers and parents kept telling him that he would never be able to write or speak unless he learned grammar. At first, with despair in his heart, he believed them, but gradually a suspicion grew that perhaps they might be wrong. Finally, in the middle of a severe lecture on his grammatical shortcomings, he interrupted the teacher and said through his tears, "When I have something to say, I can always say it!" Much later he came to the conclusion that poor speakers and writers suffered from a lack, not of grammar, but of interesting ideas, a lack that never afflicted Clarence Darrow.

Strict discipline was the rule in the schools of that era. The teacher's right to inflict physical punishment was taken for granted. Clarence's earliest school memory was associated with pain and harshness. When he was very young, before he was a regular pupil himself, he was taken to school by an older brother or sister. After sitting very still for what seemed endless hours to a little boy, he grew restless. The teacher boxed his ears, and he ran weeping from the schoolhouse. He never forgot the pain and humiliation of that day. Later on he grew accustomed to being hit as part of the regular discipline and routine of school and shrugged it off, but that first shock was to remain with him all his life. He considered it an object lesson in how hatred could be aroused by injustice and cruelty, and how punishment, instead of correcting misbehavior, usually did just the opposite. Even the mild spankings and scoldings administered by his parents produced nothing but resentment. He wondered later how people of their intelligence could not see the futility of such methods in training children.

Some of the other educational methods seemed to him just as fruitless. Along with corporal punishment and learning by rote went an emphatic repetition of moral precepts: the children were constantly urged to speak nothing but the truth, learn their lessons, love their parents, obey their teachers, be industrious, thrifty, generous, and kind, despise riches, avoid ambition, and never touch strong drink. Then all the good things of life would automatically come their way. The principal channel of these lessons was the old Mc-Guffey readers, in whose stories virtue was always rewarded and wrongdoing inevitably led to blackest doom. The children read and listened earnestly while these noble rules of conduct were funneled into them; then they went out and immediately and unthinkingly violated every one. They fought, lied, schemed, were selfish, greedy, willful, and lazy. Moreover, they saw their elders behaving in pretty much the same way, if not so openly. It never occurred to the children nor probably, thought Clarence, to their teachers either, that the precepts had any relationship to real life.

In spite of the educational shortcomings of the 1860's, Clarence enjoyed going to school. At school he met all the children of the town, and there they organized their play life, chiefly around baseball. Nothing, he wrote later, was ever to give him such unalloyed joy, nothing was ever to seem so entrancing as baseball. It was the only thing in life, he said, that came up to his hopes and expectations, and his greatest regret at growing up was that he had to give up baseball as a major activity.

The formal rules of the game had been laid down only a little more than twenty years earlier by Abner Doubleday. It had not yet become a highly organized sport with professional teams. Clarence and his friends were shocked when they later learned that there were men who played the game for money and, worse than that, actually played for towns other than their own. Playing for money seemed to them ignoble, and to play for any town but one's own was outright treachery.

There was a strong community pride in the local teams. Nothing a boy might do in his studies at school could earn him the renown and admiration that could be his on the playing field. The members of the team felt like dedicated patriots, fighting for the glory and honor of their town.

The boys practiced every minute they could snatch from the less important affairs of life. They played during the two fifteen-minute school recesses and in the one-hour lunch period, gobbling down their lunches on the way to the ball field and playing till the last ring of the school bell and the impatient exhortations of the teacher forced them back into the schoolhouse. When they were released for the day at four o'clock, they rushed home, raced through their obligatory chores, ate supper, and then tore off to the public square, which doubled as the town baseball field, where they played until it was too dark to see. Saturday was a day of pure pleasure, with nothing to disturb the long afternoon of ball-playing.

Clarence was shattered if anything interfered with a Saturday afternoon. Once there was a total eclipse of the sun right in the middle of a Saturday game. While the rest of the town regarded this marvel through bits of smoked glass, the boys gathered sadly at home plate, feeling that the heavens were deliberately conspiring against them. When at last the moon drifted far enough beyond the sun so that there was again enough light to see the ball, the boys quickly resumed playing, though they bitterly regretted the twenty minutes forever lost from their game.

As a ball park, the town square had its inconveniences. The hotel was close behind home plate; the dry-goods store was just beyond second base; and the windows of both were highly vulnerable. Not far from third base stood the biggest house in town in the middle of a large yard filled with high grass and surrounded by a grove of trees; much time was lost searching for balls in this terrain. However, there were always sure to be a good many spectators in the town square, all offering advice and encouragement. When someone really clouted the ball, the assembled crowd cheered. At crucial moments everyone in or around the square could be counted on to shout instructions to the players who, in turn, could be counted on to make enough errors to continue the high excitement.

As Clarence and his friends became proficient at baseball, they took it more seriously, and decided to form a club and wear uniforms. Mothers and sisters were drafted into making blue shirts and matching trousers coming to just below the knee, with a red stripe running down the sides. The players wore caps but no shoes or socks because they could run faster in their bare feet and because they hated to wear shoes anyway and never did except when forced to by cold weather or the formality of special occasions.

Inspired by the glamour of their uniforms, they played better ball than ever. They felt ready to challenge the teams of other towns. The boys pooled their odd-job earnings and hired a wagon drawn by a team of horses to carry them into enemy territory. Saturday afternoons were now dedicated to these intertown contests, with enthusiastic families and neighbors coming out to watch. When the game was played at home against a challenging team of special importance, the town girls would prepare a supper for the local heroes and their opponents. The high point of the day came when, at the end of the game, the home team arranged themselves on the square and gave three cheers for the opposing team, followed by three cheers for the girls.

On one of these special occasions, when the Kinsman boys were playing against their oldest and most hated rivals, things looked grim at the end of a long, hard game. It was the last half of the last inning, with two out, two runners on base, and the visiting team one run ahead. Clarence, now the team's accomplished first baseman, came to bat. He swung twice and missed, then whacked the ball hard. It sailed over the roof of the dry-goods store and rolled down to the riverbank on the other side. Before the ball could be retrieved, Clarence had circled the bases and won the game. There was a wild ovation, and that evening groups of men and boys gathered to discuss this glorious feat. For weeks the town talked of scarcely anything else, while Clarence basked in the sunlight of public acclaim. No triumph in later life, he wrote, was to prove as thrilling, and when he read of victorious Caesar being hailed on his return to Rome, he thought immediately of the great climax of his own career. Long after the deed faded away as a town topic, Clarence felt obliged to refer to it and to remind people of the time he knocked the ball over the dry-goods store and made the great home run.

There were other, though lesser, joys than baseball in Clarence's schooldays that were to linger nostalgically in his memory. To Amirus Darrow, life was serious and no human activity was more meaningful than increasing one's knowledge and wisdom. His son Clarence, however, regarded play and fun as more satisfactory than anything else life could offer. The older he grew, the more confirmed he became in this belief. He could never understand why people were always telling him that play must be put off till after work or study. That, he said, was like his mother's insistence that he eat his pie—Clarence's favorite food—not at the beginning of supper but at the end, after the meat and vegetables. He thought the best things should come first, to be sure of getting them.

When Clarence was still very young, he began to wonder why the world was so unreasonable and why parents and teachers, the rule-makers of his young world, were so lacking in kindness and imagination. Couldn't they see, he asked, that shaping life according to the rules for eating pie was dangerous? Too many people saved their pie for the last and then died before getting to it.

He started playing first thing in the morning. He set out for school early, carrying a lunch pail filled mainly with pie and cake and perhaps an apple. There was a piece of bread and butter, too, but Clarence never took this seriously and always gave it away. As the Darrow children went down the half mile to school, they were joined by others who lived along the way until they formed a boisterous, playful group, laughing and joking, chasing chipmunks, wading through the stream on warm days or sliding over it in winter. The boys went barefoot almost as soon as the snow had melted in the spring, despite the inconvenient rule of mothers that bare feet had to be washed every night before going to bed. No matter how early they left home, there was so much to do on the way to school that they were invariably late.

The early evenings, Saturdays, and all vacations were devoted chiefly to baseball, but there were other diversions offered by the still untouched country around Kinsman. There were streams where the boys went fishing, and ponds where they went swimming in the summer and ice-skating in the winter. In the summer, too, they climbed to the tops of the hills, went picnicking and berry-picking; in the fall they went nutting in the woods; in the winter they coasted down the long hillsides.

None of these pleasures, however, took place on Sundays. Sundays were different. Sundays were difficult in Kinsman. It considered itself a godly town, and games of any kind were strictly forbidden. If Clarence's own nonconformist parents did not stop him from playing, any other adult could assume the right to stop such un-Sabbath behavior.

Practically everyone went to church—except Amirus Darrow, the town agnostic. Yet Sundays were as sacred to him as to his neighbors; it was only on this day that he really, in a sense, came alive. Since all work was shut down tight on Sundays, he was able to close his woodworking shop and devote himself to his beloved books. Right after breakfast he retired to the little room set aside as his study and stayed there till far into the night, his soul thousands of miles and perhaps hundreds of years away from Kinsman and the empty drudgery of his everyday life.

Oddly enough, though Amirus and his wife did not believe in church attendance for themselves, they felt that their children should go. Every Sunday morning a reluctant Clarence had to submit to an extensive scrubbing, get dressed in his most uncomfortable clothes with a stiff collar, and, greatest hardship of all, put on stockings and heavy boots. His mother would lead the Darrow children up the hill to the United Presbyterian Church, to which most of the townspeople and neighboring farmers belonged. From early in the morning Clarence had watched the farmers drive past his house on their way to church, dressed in their best clothes, sitting stiffly and solemnly in sharp contrast to their weekday manner. He felt it was a gloomy faith and suffered through the long prayers and the longer sermons, not a word of which he understood. He could not have sat through the longest prayer of all if he had not learned to pick out landmarks as it went along. When the minister "began asking for guidance and protection for the President of the United States, it was three-quarters over, and I felt like a ship-wrecked mariner sighting land."

This same minister often came to visit Clarence's father, though Amirus himself rarely went near the church. But the two men had a close tie, nonetheless, which they shared with scarcely anyone else in town. They read and studied together, and spent long hours translating Greek.

After church services the Darrow children had to stay for Sunday school, but Clarence found this easier to bear. At least he was with his own friends and he enjoyed the singing. But the Sunday-school lessons, like the sermons, were wasted on him. He felt about them as he did about regular school lessons: they had nothing to do with his daily life or problems. The only thing he remembered later of all these lessons was how useless they seemed.

3

The Emerging Lawyer

After six years at the district school, Clarence moved on to the Kinsman public academy. Baseball was still the chief interest of the students, but other things had changed. The women teachers were replaced by men. What he considered the nightmare of English grammar was replaced by the equal nightmare of Latin grammar. Arithmetic gave way to algebra, and history was added. There were still, for a time, McGuffey's readers with their moral lessons, but on the whole, Clarence began to feel that he was leaving childhood behind him.

From the academy he went, at the age of sixteen, to Allegheny College, where he lived with the family of a professor, doing work around the house to pay for his board and room. Even with this help, however, it was a miracle how Amirus Darrow, with his small earnings, was able to scrape together enough money to send his children to college. Two of the older ones, Everett and Mary, had gone to the University of Michigan, and Amirus was determined to give the others as much education as he could manage and they could absorb.

Clarence felt that his own absorption point was rather low. At college he added the study of Greek to Latin, did poorly in both, and despised them both. He found geometry easier than algebra but considered it just as useless. The only subject that really pleased him was zoology, which awakened an enduring interest in the natural sciences. And there was still baseball. He was to say that the chief result of his higher education was to make him a better ball player.

At the end of his first year he returned home to spend the summer helping his father in the furniture shop. He found the work hard and dull, and decided that he was made for better things. He had little mechanical ability and absolutely no liking for manual labor. When he was asked later why he became a lawyer, he answered, "To escape hard work." After he became famous as a defender of labor, he used to say he would do anything for labor except engage in it.

One of the jobs assigned to him was painting furniture. Without his father knowing it, Clarence skipped the undersides of the chair seats, feeling it was a waste of his time to paint them. For years afterward, people who owned Darrow chairs used to turn them over to see if they had one painted by Clarence.

He planned to return to college at the end of the summer, but in the meantime the country had become engulfed in a financial depression. A leading banking house failed, setting off the panic of 1873. Factories shut down; unemployment spread rapidly; people stopped buying all but the barest necessities. The Darrow furniture business, small enough to begin with, dwindled to almost nothing. Clarence did not want to burden his father any longer, though Amirus urged him to continue college.

He was offered a job teaching a small district school in Vernon, about three miles from Kinsman. Though he was only seventeen, the salary was so low that the school board could scarcely expect anyone older to take it. At first his appointment was opposed by some members of the community on the ground that, as the son of a freethinker, Clarence had been exposed to dangerous ideas which he might pass on to his students. Some years earlier, his older sister Mary had been hired for the same post, only to be fired by a group of outraged parents when they realized who her father was. On the advice of a lawyer she sued the school board at the end of the year and was awarded her entire salary.

By this time, however, most of the community realized that the Darrows, though unorthodox in their churchgoing habits, were in their own way true Christians. They had won respect, if not understanding, throughout the area. Clarence himself had attended church and Sunday school, and people liked him for his easygoing nature and obvious integrity. Moreover, he had spent a whole year at college, a qualification not always found in a country schoolteacher. The dissenting parents withdrew their objections and Clarence began teaching.

The one-room, one-teacher school consisted of about fifty pupils ranging in age from seven to a year or two older than Clarence himself. It was considered a large school, and had given previous teachers a good deal of trouble. The salary was thirty dollars a month and "found." This meant that each family in a school district took turns giving the teacher room and board for one night at a time. On Fridays Clarence went back to his own home in Kinsman for the weekend. He did not mind this system of boarding around. He was always treated as company and given the best of everything, including pie and cake three times a day.

His teaching methods proved as unorthodox as his father's ideas on churchgoing. He was determined not to use corporal punishment and announced this at the very beginning, telling his students that he did not want them to do anything through fear. This was a revolutionary departure from nineteenth-century pedagogy, but Clarence felt that if he could not make his pupils wise, he would at least try to make them happy. He lengthened the lunch and recess periods, joined the children in their games, and coached them in baseball. They may not have learned much, said Clarence, but they certainly enjoyed themselves. At first the parents were disturbed, but he somehow managed to convince them that his methods were right. Even at that age, Clarence was beginning to master the art of persuasion.

Clarence had always enjoyed speaking and debating. When he was only two years old, his sister Mary began teaching him to recite little "pieces." Later on, in school, he took part in debates and public recitations. He liked listening to the discussions that went on in his father's shop. He grew used to hearing his father take the minority view, and the fact that most of the community thought differently simply deepened his conviction that his father was right. There was no doubt that Amirus brought an infinitely greater degree of learning and reflection to his arguments than did his neighbors.

Mary and Everett belonged to the local Literary Society, and long before Clarence was old enough to join himself, he went to the weekly meetings to hear the prepared essays and debates, never missing a session if he could possibly help it. Amirus encouraged him to attend and often went along with him. As soon as Clarence was old enough, he became an active member, speaking and debating with great enthusiasm.

Almost every Saturday night at the public debates held in the schoolhouse or in a large barn, Clarence Darrow, still in his teens, could be heard, generally taking the unpopular side of any debate or forum. Like his father, he never minded being one against many or on the losing side; he found any exchange of ideas, against any odds, exhilarating. Even when his listeners were openly hostile to his unconventional ideas, he was not in the least distressed but went right on, never abandoning his good-natured, gently satirical tone and never backing away from his independent views.

During the three years that he taught school and even before, Clarence spoke regularly at town forums, Fourth of July celebrations, Decoration Day services. He had no trace of shyness and enjoyed the act of speaking as much as his audience enjoyed hearing him. He dug into the preparation for a speech or debate with a willing zest that had been absent when, as a schoolboy, he lackadaisically prepared his lessons.

He had a pleasant manner and an engaging appearance. He was tall and lanky, with a large brow overhanging his deeply set blue eyes. His hair was dark and unruly; one lock always fell down over his forehead. He gave an immediate impression of candor, honesty, simplicity. The audience of townspeople and farmers liked and respected him, even though they rejected practically all of his ideas.

When Clarence was not talking himself, he took pleasure in listening to others talk. It was a period of speechmaking. Every holiday was celebrated with some kind of public ceremony, and speeches were among the principal features of the program. Political campaigns on local, state, and national levels brought forth another luxuriant crop of speakers.

Clarence soon realized that the best of these were the lawyers. Even as a young boy he had been impressed by the attorneys who came down from the county seat to address the town on public occasions. They drove fine buggies drawn by good horses; they dressed much better than the country people who came to hear them; their shoes were always shined; they spoke confidently and loudly, with dramatic gestures which Clarence admired. He decided that lawyers were great men and wondered how much money they earned, how one became a lawyer, and how much intelligence and study it took.

There was something else that stirred his interest in the law. The tinsmith, whose shop was just across the street from the Darrow house, was the justice of the peace before whom local cases were heard. Whenever a trial took place, young Clarence ran across the street to watch what he considered a great show, and followed the heated and sometimes abusive arguments of both sides with relish.

The idea of becoming a lawyer himself began to grow. After he started teaching, his enthusiasm for reading increased now that he could select the subjects himself. Every Monday morning, when he returned to school after his weekend at home, he carried along several books from his father's library. As time went on, there was generally a lawbook among them. By the end of his third year of teaching he had definitely decided to become a lawyer. In addition to its other attractions, the practice of law did not require him to work with his hands, something he was anxious to avoid.

Both Everett and Mary were teaching by this time, Everett in high school and Mary in grade school. Together with Amirus they urged him to study law at the University of Michigan, and generously offered to send him. The full course was two years, but at the end of a year he felt ready to work in a law office. This would provide the second year of training with much less expense to his family.

He found a job with a law firm in Youngstown, Ohio, some twenty miles from Kinsman. The city of twenty thousand people seemed enormous to him. At the end of a year he took the bar examination and passed. He had just turned twenty-one. When he returned home, his friends and neighbors gathered to congratulate him. No one, perhaps not even Clarence himself, was as delighted as Amirus. He believed his own life misspent, but now he felt that his son's success was his success as well.

Andover and Ashtabula

While Clarence was still teaching school, he began going out with Jessie Ohl, a young girl who lived in Berg Hill, some six miles from Kinsman, where her family owned a grist mill. The Ohls were friends of the Darrows but, unlike them, were prosperous and established. Mrs. Ohl was a woman of remarkable energy and spirit. She raised a family, managed a large wheat farm, and found time to preach in the evangelical church.

By contrast, Jessie's temperament was calm and placid. But she did have an enthusiasm for domesticity to which she brought her mother's talents.

She was the only girl in whom Clarence showed any interest as a young man. After he became a lawyer, he asked her to marry him, though at the time he had no money, no clients, and no particular prospects. Jessie, however, was perfectly willing to become the wife of a fledgling lawyer and devote herself to furthering both his well-being and career. If necessary—and at the outset it was very necessary—she would be content to live modestly and frugally, making up for the lack of money by hard work.

They established their first home—and Clarence's first real office—in Andover, about ten miles from Kinsman. Clarence would have liked to open an office in Youngstown, but he was overwhelmed by its size and importance. Andover, with only four hundred people, appeared more suitable for what he considered his modest training and ambitions. He was not interested in conventional success in terms of money or fame, feeling these might interfere with his independence.

They rented a small apartment over a shoestore and turned one room into an office. Clarence borrowed money to buy books for his small law library.

Clients were very slow in coming. In fact, the law at first seemed to pay even less than schoolteaching. To help meet expenses, Jessie rented out one room of their apartment. The boarder was a young lawyer who became Clarence's law partner as well. A few weeks later he ran up some poker debts and left town abruptly, taking Clarence's lawbooks with him.

Darrow was so young that it was hard for people to take him seriously as a lawyer. In his first case he thought he was going to demolish the opposing attorney, a much older man, and was dashed when his opponent hardly noticed him and then called him "bub" the few times he deigned to address Clarence at all.

Little by little, however, Clarence built up a practice based largely on the dairy business which was the main industry of the local farmers. He helped settle disputes over boundary lines, drew up legal documents for horse trades, and defended farmers accused of pouring water into milk to increase its volume. Sometimes his client was a farmer who had been fined for selling hard cider illegally. His fees ran from fifty cents for drawing up legal papers to five dollars for trying a case in court, though a liquor case might pay off in cider rather than in cash. He averaged about fifty to sixty dollars a month.

At the end of three years he felt he had outgrown Andover and moved to Ashtabula, the largest town in the area, with five thousand people. At about this time his son Paul was born. Clarence was now the head of a family. With this new responsibility added to the conviction that he had reached the limits of success possible in Andover, he was ready for a change.

He did not come to Ashtabula as a stranger: he had often debated and played baseball there, and had traveled to it several times in connection with cases for Andover clients. He was sufficiently well known to be elected city solicitor several months after his arrival in Ashtabula. His salary was seventy-five dollars a month, and he retained the right to take cases privately—cases which came a good deal sooner and more frequently than in Andover.

With this new affluence, he settled down to a pleasant if not exciting life. Looking back at it later, he recalled the highlights peculiar to small-town living: a horse falling down drew a crowd; a safe lowered from a second-floor window brought all traffic on Main Street to a standstill while everyone gathered to watch this novel and perhaps perilous undertaking.

Yet the practice of small-town law did have a certain excitement of its own. Any case, even a dispute between two farmers over the ownership of a cow, was sure to arouse partisan sentiment. Everyone took sides; communities, church congregations, social organizations were divided as if in a civil war. Spectators came from miles around to attend the trial, which often took on the aspect, wrote Clarence, of a medieval tournament with lawyers jousting and trying to find weak spots in their opponents' armor. Long after the trial, the merits of the case and of the decision were hashed over, leaving feuds and animosities that lingered on.

The lawyers themselves had strong personal feelings and believed that their side was unquestionably right. This was especially true of Clarence Darrow, who became so emotionally involved in his cases that fees became unimportant. Of all the legal business he handled during his Ohio days, he considered the most important a dispute over the ownership of a harness worth fifteen dollars. His client was a young boy who paid him five dollars for the first trial, which ended in the jury's disagreement. A second trial was set, but the boy had no money left. Clarence went ahead anyway, and for the next seven or eight years the case was tried, appealed, reversed, retried, appealed again, reversed again, until at last the final decision was handed down in his favor. He had spent a considerable amount of his own money in the meantime, more than he could afford, paying his client's expenses as well as his own. All he ever received in payment was the original five dollars; the harness itself cost only fifteen. These sums were only a fraction of what he spent, but he had been determined to see the case through, as though his career depended on it.

Despite the drama provided by the small-town, personal approach to law, Clarence was nevertheless oppressed from time to time by a sense of monotony and boredom. His happiest hours were those in which he could forget himself in poker, a game he enjoyed second only to baseball. There was always a game going on somewhere in town in which, with congenial friends and perhaps a drink, he could escape "the annoyances and banalities of existence."

This view of life was a matter of temperament with Darrow; it did not arise just from the slow, uneventful pace of a small town. He was to be afflicted by moods of depression even while living in one of the largest and busiest cities in the world. He felt that no halfway intelligent person could tolerate the realities of life without some form of solace or escape. For him the most satisfactory solace was the oblivion of sleep. Next best was to become so deeply absorbed in activity—any kind, no matter how frivolous—that he could be "unmindful of life." The best of these self-absorbing activities had been baseball. Now, during the years of his law practice in Ohio, he turned to poker as an avenue of escape.

Reading became another absorbing activity for Darrow. Two books in particular changed the course of his thinking.

A banker suggested that he read Henry George's *Progress and Poverty,* a book that gave Darrow new conceptions of social justice; and a police judge gave him a copy of *Our Penal Machinery and Its Victims,* by John P. Altgeld, that revolutionized his views on crime and criminals.

Henry George was one of the many reformers trying to find answers to the new social and economic problems facing the United States after the Civil War. Most of these problems were caused by the rapid transformation of America from a simple agricultural nation to a complex industrial giant at a speed which produced great social upheavals. The gap between rich and poor was rapidly growing wider. A whole new working class was created as young people left the farms and hordes of immigrants poured into the United States to fill the insatiable needs of new industries. These landless workers were poorly paid and wretchedly housed. They became the first victims of the depressions that ravaged the country at periodic intervals.

As the headaches of industrialism increased, so did the attempts to understand and cure them. Economists and political philosophers, from amateurs like Peter Cooper to professionals like Thorstein Veblen, wrote many books and pamphlets on the subject. By far the most widely read and talked-about book was Henry George's *Progress and Poverty.* It explored the paradox of why increasing material progress was accompanied by increasing poverty. The country as a whole was growing richer, but the money was becoming concentrated in the hands of fewer people, leaving more people poorer. The democratic ideal of equality was suffering in the process.

The remedy proposed by Henry George was his famous single tax on land. Through this tax, large landowners and real-estate speculators would be forced to return to the state the profits on land which they had not earned by means of their own labor. This by itself would restore economic equality. All other taxes could be abolished, to the benefit of the workers and the poor.

Henry George's ideas were enthusiastically welcomed by workers, farmers, intellectuals, and progressives throughout the world. More than two million copies of *Progress and Poverty* were sold, reaching as far as India and China. And no reader was more responsive than Clarence Darrow in Ashtabula, who felt that he had found a new political gospel.

The second influential book, *Our Penal Machinery and Its Victims*, was also an attempt to find solutions for social injustice, this time in the field of criminology. John P. Altgeld, a Chicago lawyer soon to become a judge, felt that instead of punishing crime, society should investigate its causes and then work to remove them. He criticized the current penal system, saying it did nothing to prevent crime; if anything, it made things worse. Jail did not reform an offender; it was more likely to make a habitual criminal of him. Altgeld deplored the harsh treatment of prisoners, saying "brutal treatment brutalizes, and thus prepares for crime." He felt that heredity and environment played a large part in forming criminals and noted that most of them came from among the poor and unfortunate. Like Henry George, he was concerned with the problem of poverty and the effects upon its victims. In his book he outlined a series of specific prison reforms. Again like Henry George, he combined sympathy for the underdog with a rational approach to the ills of society.

Most of the professional reviewers ignored the book or dismissed it as well-meant, conscientiously prepared, but too visionary. Altgeld realized that if he wanted to spread his ideas and effect any reforms, he would have to promote the book himself. He mailed more than ten thousand free copies to public officials, writers, clergymen, and other men of influence throughout the country. One of these was the police magistrate in Ashtabula, who passed his copy on to the young lawyer Clarence Darrow.

The book came to Darrow as a revelation, leading to a complete reversal of his ideas on crime. Before this, he had taken the conventional view of a criminal as someone who deliberately chose to be evil. That the criminal might be not the enemy of society but its victim had never occurred to him. *Our Penal Machinery and Its Victims* became his guide; and not only the book but its author, John Altgeld, were to exert a profound influence upon his career.

Darrow did fairly well in Ashtabula and might have been content to spend the rest of his life there, if a trivial and irrelevant incident had not jolted him out of it. When he was thirty years old, he decided to buy a house. He had saved up five hundred dollars. He and Jessie went house-hunting, found a place they liked, and agreed to buy it for thirty-five hundred dollars. Clarence drew up a deed of sale, agreeing to pay five hundred in cash and the rest in monthly payments over several years. The owner took the deed home, to return it the next day with his own and his wife's signatures. But when he returned, he confessed that he could not sell the house because his wife refused to sign the deed. She doubted Clarence's ability to keep up the payments.

Clarence was furious. "All right, I don't want your house because—," he thought frantically for a reason, "—because— I'm going to move away from here."

The next day he met another woman with whom he was not on friendly terms. She asked him sarcastically how he was doing and he replied that he was doing very well. In fact, he improvised, he had just gotten a big case in Chicago and was going to try it there the next morning.

The next morning he took an early train to Chicago to avoid meeting the woman on the streets of Ashtabula. If she saw him in town, she might, said Clarence, "have told the whole town I was a liar—which I was."

In Chicago he went to see his brother Everett, who was teaching there. Everett, with his intelligence and generosity, was respected by the younger members of the family, who always went to him for advice and assistance. He advised Clarence to make his story about moving come true by settling in Chicago. He felt that Clarence was wasting his talents in Ashtabula and needed the range and stimulation of the larger city. Clarence hesitated—all he had was the five hundred dollars with which he had planned to buy the house—but Everett offered to help him with additional money.

Clarence decided to move to Chicago, though it looked "big and lonely." This was a vitally important step in his life, yet it was due entirely to a woman's arbitrary refusal to sign a deed of sale. In later discussions with friends, Darrow said this incident proved the absence of free will. A man's life, he claimed, was determined by a series of meaningless accidents. What, he would ask, would have happened if that woman had signed? "I would probably be in Ashtabula now, in a little law office, trying to meet overdue payments."

He saw no pattern in life, no over-all purpose. Everything was due to pure chance, and it was just chance that now brought him to the main arena in which he was to perform so brilliantly and to such good purpose.

5

Chicago

If any one city exemplified America's industrial coming-of-age, with its raw vigor, magnificent technical achievements, and appalling social maladjustments, it was the Chicago of the 1880's to which Darrow came. No city in the United States had grown more rapidly or more furiously and unevenly than Chicago.

Before the opening of the Erie Canal in 1825, it was largely an Indian village, with a few white traders and some officers from nearby Fort Dearborn. The opening of the canal brought a great movement of trade, traveling both east and west, and of westward migrants. Many of these decided to settle in Chicago instead of continuing their journey. In 1848 the Illinois-Michigan Canal was opened, so that now the town was at the junction of the two chief water routes of the United States: the Great Lakes, connecting with the eastern seaboard through the Erie Canal, and the Mississippi River system which linked Chicago with the important towns of St. Louis and New Orleans. It became the country's largest inland port, the chief transmission point for manufactured goods from the east, grain and livestock from the west, lumber from the north.

The coming of the railroads accelerated these busy currents. Chicago soon became the principal midway station of the overland routes—the great central market of the United States. It continued to grow rapidly until it became the biggest railroad terminal, the leading grain market, and the most important livestock and meat-packing center in the world.

The booming young city provided unlimited opportunities, which drew ambitious young men, shrewd entrepreneurs, adventurers and speculators of all kinds like flies to a honeypot. New industries multiplied and created the need for still other industries which in turn drew more people to Chicago. The new inhabitants needed homes, furniture, utilities, all of which made the circle of needs and growth spin at a dizzily increasing speed. Property values skyrocketed. In 1830 the first town lots had sold for forty dollars. In 1844 a piece of land was bought for eight thousand dollars and sold eight years later for three million dollars. Men became millionaires overnight. In Darrow's time, there were more than two hundred millionaires in the city, nearly all self-made.

The mad scramble for money produced a society in which worth was measured crudely in terms of wealth. Yet along with the greed and the jungle competition went a surprising awakening of culture. A magnificent new auditorium was built to house the new symphony orchestra and opera company. This was followed by the Art Institute, for which a prize collection was quickly assembled, and by the establishment of the University of Chicago where new educational frontiers were explored, like John Dewey's famous experimental elementary school.

New literary movements arose, especially in the form of the "little magazine," like *The Dial,* and the specialized newspaper column, like Eugene Field's "Sharps and Flats." *The Dial* had its headquarters in the Fine Arts Building which also housed the Little Theater, the first of its kind in the United States, together with a whole galaxy of writers' and artists' groups. Soon there would be an even greater flowering when novelists and poets like Theodore Dreiser, Upton Sinclair, Sherwood Anderson, Edgar Lee Masters, Vachel Lindsay, Floyd Dell, and Carl Sandburg appeared on the Chicago scene.

The outstanding aesthetic expression of the burgeoning city, however, was its architecture. Chicago led the rest of the country in the construction of the modern skyscraper, made possible by the development of cheap steel beams and the electric elevator. Another factor in the creation of the skyscraper was the economic need to crowd as many business offices as possible onto a given piece of expensive land in the commercial section of the city. With buildings going high into the air, the same piece of precious ground could hold many more offices than the old horizontal structures, and the owner could collect far more rent from his property.

The architectural form was thus determined in part by the function of the building, in part by the new structural materials available. It was a direct reflection of the life of Chicago, with its strong commercial interests and high land values. In these respects it carried out the ideas of Louis Sullivan, the leader and chief spokesman of the Chicago school of architecture. He insisted that buildings must not imitate the designs of the past, but must suit the needs of their own age. A warehouse should look like a warehouse, not like a medieval castle. His phrase, "Form follows function," became the keynote of the new architecture. Together with his famous disciple, Frank Lloyd Wright, he exerted a tremendous and original influence upon American design.

The city to which Darrow came already bore this new imprint. The great fire of 1871, which destroyed more than two thousand acres, had given the architects of Chicago a unique opportunity to rebuild the city along modern lines, developing the skyscraper as a fusion of aesthetics and function, and as an expression of the commercial spirit of the age. The disturbing fact that the new tall buildings cut off air and sunlight from the narrow streets below, and brought great crowds of people into a limited area, was in itself another symptom of the new age. The industrial revolution brought both progress and ugliness; it liberated some men and enslaved others; it solved technological problems and created social ones.

Chicago was the complicated, confused, bustling vortex of this new era. The rough frontier town had turned into a sophisticated metropolis with alternating patches of rawness and culture, extreme wealth and devastating poverty. Along with the opulent and thriving rich were masses of wretched poor. Thousands of railroad, stockyard, and factory workers, mostly foreign-born, were shockingly overworked and underpaid, with no security or protection of any kind. While Chicago's leading merchant, Marshall Field, was spending seventy-five thousand dollars on his son's birthday party, poor children were receiving less than thirty-five cents for a twelve-hour working day. If a worker was injured in an industrial accident, of which there were a great many before the era of safety regulations, he was turned out into the street without compensation. The principle of social responsibility on the part of the community had not yet been accepted. Defensive action by labor itself through strikes or unions was opposed with repressive violence.

The uneven development of the city could be seen everywhere. The rich built ornate mansions along the beautiful shore of Lake Michigan while the poor crowded miserably into substandard hovels in filthy slums. A cultivated, urban way of life was emerging, yet most of the streets remained unpaved, turning into mud under rains and heavy traffic. The Chicago River was polluted with industrial and human wastes, and typhoid was widespread. The elaborately decorated homes of the wealthy and the dark, airless alleys of the workers were equally assailed by the stench rising from the cattle yards and slaughterhouses.

It was a maelstrom of a city: cruel, dangerous, heartless, corrupt; yet at the same time vigorous, exciting, stimulating. There were endless opportunities for success or failure; there was room for everyone—to be nourished by the rich current of life or overwhelmed by the gigantic odds that could quickly pile up against the undefended.

Darrow's first year in Chicago was discouraging. He could not afford his own office but rented desk space in someone else's. He had few friends in Chicago and no connections that might bring in clients. During that entire first year he earned only about three hundred dollars and was forced to borrow money to meet expenses.

He suffered from loneliness and missed the easy sociability of life in Ashtabula and Kinsman. "A cloud of homesickness," he wrote, "hung over me." He would walk along the street or stand on a busy corner staring at faces, hoping to see someone from Ohio. Even if all his Ohio associates came to Chicago en masse, he reflected gloomily, they would have been lost in that surging crowd hurrying through the streets.

In search of new contacts he joined the Henry George Single Tax Club, where debates and talks were held at regular weekly meetings. After a few sessions he, too, began to talk, "so that I would not completely forget how to form sentences and feel at home on my feet." As in his early days of public speaking in Ohio, his listeners warmed to him, and he began at last to make friends in his new city.

His ability as a speaker was quickly recognized, and soon he was asked to make speeches for the Democratic party in the election campaign of 1888. The Darrow family had been Democrats ever since Horace Greeley, the idealistic editor of the influential New York *Tribune*, had run for President against General Grant, the Republican candidate. In this, as in everything else, they differed from the rest of their town, and young Clarence grew accustomed to political controversy from the very start.

At the political rallies in Chicago, he was only one of a long string of young and ambitious lawyers, all anxious to make their voices heard and to further their careers. As a newcomer, Clarence was generally one of the last speakers, by which time the audience had stopped listening, or he would be interrupted by the candidates themselves who arrived at the end of each meeting. Upon their arrival, the audience would rise and cheer and in the noisy confusion would forget all about the speaker on the platform.

But his skill as a speaker continued to attract attention, and he was occasionally asked to address a civic meeting. At one of these he was to appear on the same platform with a popular senator. When Darrow entered the hall, he was delighted to see that it was completely filled, with at least half a dozen newspaper reporters sitting in front. He had long been hoping for some notice from the newspapers, but so far they had ignored him. Now, he felt, his chance had come. He made what he considered a good speech, received some applause, then yielded the platform to the senator, who was greeted with wild cheers.

The next day the newspapers were filled with reports of the senator, but there was not one word about Clarence. He was acutely disappointed. Throughout the first half of his life, he wrote later, he was eager to get into the news; throughout the last half he was just as eager to keep out of it. This was still the first half of his life, and he was filled with gloom at failing to attract even a shred of public notice.

He despaired of achieving any kind of success in Chicago. If he had had any money at all, he would have returned to Ohio. But he could go back only if he borrowed money, and this would mean admitting defeat, which he could not bring himself to do. He remained in Chicago, sunk in discouragement. He had not yet learned, he said, to accept whatever came along and "not take either gratification or disappointment too seriously." Nor had he yet discovered, as he did later, the truth of Bret Harte's comment that the only sure thing about luck is that it will change.

The change was not long in coming. He was asked to speak at the final session of a huge free-trade convention. Henry George had come to Chicago to address the meeting and the house was packed with every single-taxer in the area, together with a great crowd who had come just to get a look at the famous man. George was the first speaker and captured the audience so completely that when he was through everyone rose to leave, feeling the rest of the program would be an anticlimax. Darrow urged the chairman to introduce him quickly, and his friends in the auditorium tried to rouse interest by applauding the introduction enthusiastically.

Darrow knew that unless he could capture this reluctant audience with his first few words, his talk would be a failure. He frantically searched for striking phrases and began his speech on the most vivid note he could think of. The audience, which had expected nothing of this relatively unknown speaker, paused, their interest aroused. Gradually, as he went on talking, they began to sit down again, one after another. Darrow knew a great deal about free trade and had prepared his address carefully. Soon he had everyone's rapt attention. He looked down and saw the newspapermen listening closely and taking notes on what he was saying.

An "exquisite thrill of triumph" swept through him; he felt he could sway his listeners as he wished. He relaxed and began to feel as easy and confident as though, he said, he were sitting by his own fireside with old friends, free to say whatever he pleased. This was the beginning of the famous Darrow style. Up to this time he had used the florid oratorical approach so popular in that era, embellished with clouds of elaborate rhetoric. But now, as he gained confidence, he stopped trying for effects and spoke simply and directly to his attentive listeners.

At the end of his speech there was tremendous applause. Henry George shook his hand warmly; people came up to ask questions. The next morning he was gratified to see his name on the front pages of the newspapers. During the day people dropped in to his office to congratulate him on his speech. He was invited to take part in the election campaign of DeWitt Cregier for mayor, but this time he was given his choice of fellow speakers. Darrow said he would speak alone, with no one else on the program. He had had enough of close-quarter competition.

DeWitt Cregier himself had been in the audience that night and had marked Clarence Darrow as a promising man. When he was elected mayor, he thought of Darrow for a job on his new staff. His decision was based not only on his own impressions but also on the strong recommendation of a political colleague, Superior Court Judge John P. Altgeld.

Clarence had gone to see Altgeld soon after coming to Chicago, taking with him Altgeld's book, *Our Penal Machinery and Its Victims,* which had stirred him back in Ashtabula. A warm, close relationship between the two men was inevitable. Though very different in temperament, they shared the same views.

Altgeld, ten years older than Darrow, became his life-long friend. He influenced the younger man's ideas and guided his career, and was in turn helped in his political activities by Darrow. In their first interview Altgeld asked him a great many questions about himself and then offered to help in any way possible.

What Darrow needed most of all was clients. After his speech at the free-trade convention, Chicago no longer seemed so enormous or so cold. He was gaining recognition, friends, a place inside the workings of the metropolis. He joined a literary club and began giving talks on literature. He wrote articles for liberal publications. But he was still unable to earn enough money. He had wanted newspaper publicity largely because he thought it would attract clients, but his office remained almost as empty as before. He spent more time making free speeches than doing paid legal work.

A little more than two months after his speech, he received a letter from Mayor Cregier asking him to call when he had the time. Darrow, sitting in his dismally empty office, thought ruefully that he had nothing but time and went to see the mayor at once.

When Cregier offered him the position of special assessment attorney at a salary of three thousand dollars a year, Darrow could hardly believe it. He accepted on the spot and, since he had practically no business of his own to wind up, began working for the city immediately.

On the strength of his suddenly bright prospects, he and Jessie moved out of the modest apartment in which they had been living and leased a house instead. Jessie, cautious as ever, rented out the top floor of the new house as a bulwark against financial overconfidence.

The confidence was justified, however. Three months after Darrow started working for the city, the assistant corporation counsel resigned after a political quarrel, and Darrow was given the job at five thousand dollars a year. Ten months later, the acting corporation counsel became ill, and Clarence was again promoted to the vacant place. He was now, at the age of thirty-three, head of the legal department of the city of Chicago.

6

The Haymarket Bomb

For the next few years Darrow was kept busy with the affairs of the city of Chicago. In the course of his work he came to know every Chicago judge, alderman, and most of the politicians. He spent a good deal of time in court, gaining invaluable experience in trial procedures and techniques, laying the groundwork for one of his most famous qualities: his almost uncanny knowledge of how judges and juries could be expected to react.

He often had to make quick decisions with no time for preliminary study and, in making these, followed his own intuitive judgment. He found that his solutions, even when hardly more than guesses, were nearly always right. At the time, Darrow thought his own wisdom had led to the right answers, but later on he came to believe that the courts decided in his favor not because of any superior ability on

his part, but because he was working for a large and powerful city. It was the tendency of courts, he felt, to rule in
favor of organized society against the individual. Nevertheless, whether it was wisdom, powerful backing, or just plain
luck that proved him right, the habit of following his own
convictions regardless of precedent or current practice became permanently ingrained.

His experience in municipal government began to change
his political ideas. He no longer agreed with Henry George
and the single-taxers. The problems of the world now
seemed to him much too complex for the simple remedies
they proposed.

He was left without any formal political faith, though he
considered himself something of a radical. He was opposed
to the injustice of the present system and felt that the state
often oppressed the individual, but he could not offer any
specific program for improvement. He wanted to keep society flexible and mobile, and he wanted "a fairer distribu-
tion of this world's goods." Of the major political parties,
he considered the Democratic party closer to these aims,
so he supported it though he had few illusions about it.

It was futile, he believed, to search for a perfect system
of government. There could be no such thing, he felt, because human beings were not fixed, static units that could
be regulated by a fixed, static system. Each man was a
separate entity, with his own unique combination of fears,
hopes, motivations, and needs; a government that might
serve one man well might be bad for another. No social or
political system should be regarded as perfect or sacred
and hence not to be criticized or changed. He had only one

suggestion to offer for the improvement of society: everyone, he wrote, should be taught to be sympathetic, tolerant, and reasonable—and added in the next sentence that this in itself is a hopeless task.

Darrow himself regarded the world with a high degree of sympathy, tolerance, and reason. He kept his mind open in a kind of freewheeling attitude that led him to accept truth only tentatively. An idea was right or true only until it was disproved or replaced with something that seemed more true. No idea was allowed to harden in his own mind into a fixed opinion. He once said, "I am sure of very little and I shouldn't be surprised if those things were wrong." Like his father, he constantly questioned and reexamined and disputed. He was an almost professional disagreer. When he was with a group of conservatives, he argued like a radical. When he was with radicals, he poked holes in their theories and sounded like a conservative.

On the whole, he was for what he called "minority people," and he held "minority views." He was for the individual against the majority or the state, for the worker against the large corporation. He made no secret of his political ideas or his sympathy with labor, and expressed these views in many public speeches.

Yet he was respected and sought after by the very kind of "big business" he criticized. After some three years of working for the city, he was offered a job by the Chicago and Northwestern Railroad, an organization he had opposed in the courts. As corporation counsel of Chicago, he had successfully fought the railroads' opposition to opening certain of the city's streets across the railroads' right-of-way. Nevertheless, despite their defeat at his hands and despite their knowledge of his social views, the directors of the Chicago and Northwestern were so impressed by his ability that they asked him to be their general attorney.

At first he hesitated, feeling that this kind of law practice went against the grain of his beliefs, but finally, and chiefly on the advice of John Altgeld, he accepted. Financially, it was a happy step. The salary was seven thousand dollars a year. He and Jessie were able to buy an attractive house on Chicago's north side.

His associates at the railroad gave him their unreserved friendship and respect. Yet he remained uneasy and never really enjoyed his position. He found it hard to take the side of the railroads against an injured worker or passenger.

Somehow he managed to maintain a tentative equilibrium between his work and his sympathies. Though employed by the railroads, whose labor policies were notoriously harsh, he retained his contact with labor organizations and took part in many liberal activities. The most important example of this was his leadership of the movement to free the Haymarket anarchists.

The Haymarket affair was the violent climax of the struggle that had been going on between workers and employers since the 1870's. The first outbreak had been the great strike of '77: railroad workers, supported by an army of unemployed and desperate men, victims of the financial panic of 1873 and its long aftermath, left their jobs in protest against a second cut of ten per cent in wages that were already at starvation point. Pitched battles took place between the militia and workers in many industrial cities, and order had to be restored by federal troops. Subsequent strikes and riots, though less violent, added to the hatred, fear, and suspicion on both sides.

In 1886 the big issue was the eight-hour day. Four hundred thousand workers joined in the movement to cut the working day from ten or twelve hours to eight. A general strike was set for May first. In Chicago there were already fifty thousand men striking in dozens of industries, and the city felt menaced and fearful as May first approached. Inflammatory newspaper editorials, labeling the eight-hour movement as "foreign" and "un-American," and extensive police mobilization added to the atmosphere of panic.

Chicago was by then the labor capital of the country, the center of the worker-employer struggle. In no other American city was the pursuit of money so rampant and unchecked; in no other city was the exploitation of labor so ruthless. And nowhere else were the rich so conspicuously rich or the poor so oppressively poor.

On May first, eighty thousand Chicago workers left their jobs; yet the day passed peacefully enough. Two days later, however, trouble broke out at the McCormick reaper plant, which had dismissed all workers belonging to unions. Police fired into the crowd, killing four men and wounding many others.

A group of anarchists called a protest meeting in the Haymarket, a large square that could hold more than twenty thousand people. At least this number was expected, but the weather turned cold and threatening, and only three thousand, including women and children, showed up. After a few hours of speeches, the crowd dwindled to less than a thousand. During the last speech it began to rain and more people left. The mayor, who had come to check on the situation personally, was convinced that the affair was peaceable and went home, stopping off on his way at the nearby police station where a riot squad had been held ready in case of trouble. The captain in charge was told to dismiss the squad; but, after the mayor left, the hot-tempered captain decided to take matters into his own hands and marched to the meeting at the head of his force. He ordered the remaining listeners to disperse at once. The speaker, just a few minutes from his conclusion, protested. While the speaker and the captain were arguing, a sputtering object was seen flying through the air. It was a bomb, the first to be used against human beings in the United States. It exploded in the front ranks of the police, who immediately began shooting. Some of the workers were armed and fired back. In a matter of seconds there was bloody pandemonium in the square.

In two or three minutes it was all over. Seven policemen had been killed and sixty-seven wounded, many by bullets rather than the bomb. A high police official declared later that many of the police had been shot by each other's wildly aimed guns. It was impossible to know how many workers were killed or wounded because they were at once carried away from the scene by their panicking friends.

It was a disaster in every way. An intense wave of anti-labor hysteria spread through the country, undoing years of slow, painful progress by labor organizations. People began to associate labor with violence and criminal behavior, and talked fearfully of revolution. Legislatures hastened to pass antilabor laws, and courts proceeded with equal haste to convict union members of conspiracy and rioting. Newspaper editorials demanded immediate action.

The police lost no time in arresting eight anarchist leaders, five of whom had not even gone to the Haymarket that night. The police knew that none of these men had hurled the bomb; instead, they were charged with inciting, through their speeches and writings, some unknown person to throw it. There was no evidence to connect the defendants with the bomb-thrower, whose identity remains unknown to this day.

The jurors, who had been picked from a special panel and had openly admitted prejudice against the defendants, found them all guilty. Seven were sentenced to death; the eighth, to the penitentiary for fifteen years.

There was jubilation over the verdict, especially in the press. But many people, particularly lawyers, expressed misgivings over the conduct of the trial and the flimsiness of the evidence on which the men had been convicted. An Amnesty Association was formed to fight the executions. During the long months of legal stays and appeals, public opinion began to shift toward the men. Finally two of them had their sentences commuted to life imprisonment. A third committed suicide by chewing a tiny percussion cap which had been smuggled to him in a cigar. The other four were hanged in November, 1887.

The Amnesty Association now bent its efforts to getting pardons for the three men still alive. The leaders of the

Association were George Schilling, one of the principal labor leaders of Chicago, Henry Demarest Lloyd, a liberal writer and speaker, and Clarence Darrow. Schilling, like Darrow, had found John Altgeld's book a revelation. He, too, had met the author and had become his close friend and political supporter. Shortly after the Haymarket trial, Altgeld had been elected judge on the Democratic ticket with the endorsement of Schilling's United Labor Party. "What ought to be done now," said Darrow, "is to take a man like Judge Altgeld, first elect him mayor of Chicago, then governor of Illinois." With Altgeld as governor, Darrow thought, the release of the men would be certain.

Six years after the Haymarket bombing, Altgeld was elected governor of Illinois. Darrow and his friends thought the release of the prisoners should be the governor's first official act and told him so; but month after month passed while Altgeld attended to other matters that he considered more pressing.

Altgeld's delay was partly the result of an acute personal dilemma. To achieve success, he had had to overcome every kind of obstacle: the extreme poverty and ignorance of his German peasant parents, severe physical handicaps including a harelip and a series of debilitating illnesses, devastating financial and political setbacks. These early struggles had darkened his temper, but had also left him with a sense of compassionate identification with the downtrodden. He shared this last quality with Darrow; it was one reason for the strong attraction between the two men.

Altgeld, however, also had a driving ambition to succeed in politics, whereas Darrow never wanted any kind of political office, saying that he enjoyed political problems but disliked political life. Altgeld was fascinated by it; he once said that politics gave him the excitement and recreation which other men derived from gambling or horse racing. And having once entered public life, he marshaled his tremendous energies to rise as rapidly and as high as he could.

This led to a painful conflict between his rigid sense of justice and his equally rigid political ambitions. Until now, he had moved cautiously. He said the time to fight injustice was after one had gained the power to take effective action. If he revealed his feelings too early, he would spoil his chances to gain this necessary power. If he talked the way he felt, he told George Schilling, "I could not be where I am. I want to do something, not just make a speech."

But now he had the power and was not doing anything about the Haymarket prisoners. To release the prisoners would arouse serious antagonism among the powerful business interests that controlled Illinois and might ruin his career. Political expediency demanded that he shut his eyes to the Haymarket prisoners as former governors had done; justice and humanity demanded with equal strength that he grant a pardon. While his supporters waited anxiously to see which course he would take, Altgeld did nothing, said nothing.

After several months Darrow began to wonder if he had been mistaken in Altgeld. Where were the humanity, honesty, and courage he had admired in the older man? He went to see the governor and expressed his impatience and doubts. He and his friends, he said, could see no excuse for the delay. "Go and tell your friends," replied Altgeld, "that when I am ready I will act. I don't know how I will act, but I will do what I think is right."

When Darrow showed his irritation over this disappointing speech, Altgeld continued:

"We have been friends for a long time. . . . I know how you feel, but this responsibility is mine. I will do what I believe to be right, no matter what that is. But don't deceive yourself: If I conclude to pardon those men it will not meet with the approval that you expect; let me tell you that from that day I will be a dead man politically."

Altgeld was right. When, after carefully studying the documents, he granted the pardon, there was an immediate outburst of venomous condemnation. Clarence Darrow had known there were thousands of people who would applaud the action; what he had underestimated were the millions who regarded it as monstrous. Altgeld was attacked as a traitor, "an apologist for murder," a "fomenter of lawlessness." His foreign birth—he had been brought to America at the age of three months—was thrown up against him; he was accused of being an "un-American anarchist," who by his action was encouraging the overthrow of civilization. Yet Altgeld, by then a very rich man with large real-estate holdings, was no more an anarchist than any other big businessman.

He made it clear that he was pardoning the men not out of sympathy or clemency—if they were guilty and had been tried fairly they would deserve the punishment, he said—but for a strictly legal reason: the trial had been grossly unfair, based on insufficient evidence, and held before a packed jury and a prejudiced judge. But this was exactly what aroused the press and the leaders of industry and politics. Altgeld had raised the shocking possibility that the government, through its courts and judges, could be unjust and in error. His pardon statement was considered an outright attack on the country's sacred institutions. In the next decade reformers and muckrakers would make similar exposures. At the moment, however, Altgeld was very much alone, with only a few friends like Clarence Darrow and George Schilling to stand by him against the barrage of slander and accusation.

Even the usual hangers-on at the state capitol melted away, leaving the great building, wrote Darrow, barren and deserted. After the pardon Darrow went to visit Altgeld as often as he could, sitting in silence with the lonely man, "just to be with him." Altgeld had acted according to his beliefs at the expense of his political career, and for the rest of his life, John "Pardon" Altgeld, as his enemies now called him, would suffer for it.

7

---◆◀●---

The Right to Strike: Pullman

Not long after the Haymarket pardon, Clarence Darrow himself, like Altgeld, had to choose between principles and career. In 1894 one of the bitterest struggles between labor and management broke out, with the railway workers on one side and the railway owners on the other. As attorney for the Chicago and Northwestern Railroad Company, Darrow's interests lay on the side of the owners; his sympathies, however, were with the workers.

It must be remembered that labor conditions were vastly different in Darrow's period from what they became half a century later. The powerful position of labor unions today would have seemed like the wildest Utopian dream back in the 1890's. Conditions which are taken for granted today—reasonable working hours, a living wage, compensation for accidents, provision for unemployment and old age, the very right to organize—were then considered outrageous demands and hotly contested by employers. Government laws and regulations, which today give as much support to labor as to management, were in that period heavily weighted in favor of management. At a time when it was dangerous to his career to do so, Darrow joined the fight that was to transform the exploited worker of the 1890's into the secure, well-paid union member of today.

Until the 1890's most unions had been set up according to craft. The railroad workers, for example, were split up into Brotherhoods, a different one for each kind of job: engineers, locomotive firemen, switchmen, trainmen, yardmasters, railroad conductors, and so on, each with their own separate organization. Unskilled workers had no union at all and were looked down upon by the skilled elite. There was no cooperation between the Brotherhoods; they often fought each other, sometimes to the extent of helping an employer destroy a rival Brotherhood.

Eugene V. Debs, an officer of the Brotherhood of Locomotive Firemen, felt that railroad workers would never be able to bargain successfully with their employers as long as they were broken up into separate, warring groups. It became his dream to unify the workers into one single, strong industrial union.

He realized his dream in 1893 when he organized the American Railway Union, one of the first industrial unions in the history of American labor. Workers in every branch of railroading eagerly joined. In the spring of 1894, when it carried through the first strike ever won against a major railroad, thousands of new members signed up. In June of that same year, the ARU held its first convention. At one of the sessions, a committee of workers from the Pullman Company appeared and begged the union for help.

They were casualties of the 1893 panic. In that year the stock market had crashed again, setting off one of the worst depressions in American history. Again, thousands of banks and businesses failed; factories cut production drastically or closed down altogether; tens of thousands of workers were thrown out of work or had their wages cut. There was suffering and starvation, with no form of government relief. Unemployed workers roamed through the country in a futile attempt to find work and stay alive.

Among the depression victims were the employees of the Pullman Palace Car Company. They lived in the extraordinary town of Pullman, the first model industrial company town in America. It had been built by George M. Pullman, the ingenious inventor of the Pullman sleeping car. These cars were not sold to the railroads; they were attached to regular trains but operated by his own company, an immensely profitable procedure.

As the company expanded, George Pullman's fertile mind conceived a new idea in industrial relations. Like other large employers of labor, he had been troubled by the unrest and dissatisfaction of his workers and by their attempts to organize unions. These problems, he decided, could be avoided by providing an atmosphere from which "unhealthy" influences would be firmly excluded. He would build a model town which would encourage model workers. He built his Utopia just south of Chicago. There were tree-shaded, well-paved streets lined with row houses, parks and flower beds, a miniature lake for boating and swimming, facilities for every athletic and cultural activity, including a theater, a library, and a church.

The life of the town was regulated by George Pullman's strict principles of hard work, sobriety, and a fair profit. No liquor was allowed, not even the occasional glass of beer to which most of the workers had been accustomed. Any sign of interest in a union was immediately punished by the loss of one's job. Political activity was limited to voting for company-approved candidates at the instruction of the shop foremen. George Pullman was a Republican and anyone openly campaigning for a Democrat ran into trouble. Close tabs were kept on everyone by means of informers who were present everywhere.

Above all, the town had to show a profit. Every Pullman worker had to rent a Pullman house, though rents were at least twenty-five per cent higher than anywhere else. Gas and water also cost more; the Pullman Company bought these from Chicago and resold them to its tenants at a higher rate. All food and supplies had to be bought in Pullman stores; money had to be kept in the Pullman bank. The library, equipped with a gift of five thousand books from George Pullman, charged annual dues that few families could afford. The rent for the one church in town was so high that the Presbyterians who used it for a few years went bankrupt. After that, no other congregation tried to meet the heavy charge.

The whole town of about twelve thousand inhabitants, mostly foreign-born, was a kind of feudal domain with

George Pullman as its overlord. A Pullman worker once said: "We are born in a Pullman house, fed from the Pullman shop, taught in the Pullman school, catechized in the Pullman church, and when we die we shall be buried in the Pullman cemetery and go to the Pullman hell."

George Pullman was an excellent businessman as well as a successful inventor. His company was so soundly managed that it could have weathered the depression of 1893 easily; it could have paid the usual dividends out of the large untouched surplus that had piled up over the years. But Pullman was not satisfied with just outlasting the depression; he wanted to keep profits up to their normal level. So when orders for new railway cars began to fall off, he reduced his overhead by drastic wage cuts and layoffs. He reduced his cash outlay for labor so much that he was able not only to maintain profits but actually to increase them.

But what of the workers? Their wages had been cut in some departments by as much as seventy per cent. Yet the rents on Pullman houses were kept at the same level, though rents in neighboring towns had dropped as much as thirty per cent because of the depression. Pullman refused to lower his rents, saying that the Pullman Land Company had no connection with the Pullman Palace Car Company. The Land Company had to earn its regular profits regardless of how little the employees of the Palace Car Company might be getting. Since rents were deducted from wages in advance, some workers found as little as seven cents left in their pay envelopes on which to feed their families. Others found no cash at all, only a notice of how much they owed the company.

In the spring of 1894, after a terrible winter, the workers asked company officials for permission to send a delegation to discuss their unbearable situation. Permission was given, together with a promise that the delegates would not be discharged. Forty-three men were chosen. While they were talking with the vice-president of the company, George Pullman burst into the room and said there was nothing to discuss. The next day all forty-three were fired and their families thrown out of the company houses.

In desperation the workers decided to strike. At the end of the first month, they went to the convention of the American Railway Union and appealed for help. The convention delegates, moved by the stories of how strikers' families had been evicted from their Pullman homes and their credit cut off at Pullman stores, offered to stop work on trains that carried Pullman cars. But Debs was reluctant to take such strong measures. Instead, he made two attempts to arbitrate.

George Pullman refused to see either the union representatives or his own workers, saying there was nothing to arbitrate. Public officials and newspapers all over the country urged Pullman to reconsider. They feared that a major strike during a tense depression period might have dangerous results. Even Mark Hanna, the powerful political boss of the Republican party, sent an emissary to Pullman asking him to arbitrate. When Pullman still refused, Mark Hanna exploded: "The damned idiot . . . What does he think he's doing! A man who won't meet his men halfway is a damned fool!"

The ARU strike began and at first appeared to be successful. Railroad traffic was tied up from Chicago to the Pacific Coast.

Strong countermeasures were now taken by the General Managers Association—an organization of Western railroad operators, including Clarence Darrow's employers, whose main purpose was to fight labor unions. They saw the situation as an opportunity to destroy Debs's industrial union before it became too powerful.

They recruited strikebreakers to run the trains. Then they turned to United States Attorney General Richard Olney, who arranged for an injunction against the union leaders. This was a court order forbidding them to take any further part in the strike; they could no longer direct or even talk or write about it. If the leaders obeyed the injunction, the Pullman strike would collapse; if they disobeyed, they would be jailed for contempt. Debs decided to ignore the injunction and continue the strike.

Olney now persuaded President Cleveland to send federal troops to break the strike. On July fourth the troops entered Chicago and set up camp on the lake front. With the soldiers came several thousand specially appointed marshals armed and paid by the railroads. Many of these were hastily recruited and were described by the Chicago police as "thugs, thieves, and ex-convicts."

Governor Altgeld was furious. He sent an indignant wire to President Cleveland saying that the action was unnecessary, since the Illinois state militia could handle any violence that might occur, and unconstitutional, since no federal issue was involved and federal troops can be used in a state matter only on application of the governor or legislature. A curt exchange of telegrams followed, with Cleveland insisting that he had the right to protect the United States mail carried on the trains. Other governors joined Altgeld in protesting what they considered illegal interference by the federal government in state affairs.

The citizens of Chicago resented the presence of the troops as much as Altgeld and the strikers did. When soldiers and marshals tried to move the trains, acting as strikebreakers, an angry mob gathered. Every tough and derelict element in Chicago joined the crowd—members of the underworld, street gangs, homeless vagrants, men who knew little and cared less about the original basis of the conflict. It had been a hard depression year, and its victims had reached the breaking point.

The railroad owners were determined to move the trains; the crowd was equally determined to prevent them. Now, for the first time, violence really erupted. Railroad cars were burned; tracks were blocked; rioting broke out. The special marshals fired into the crowd, killing several men. According to the police, these marshals also stole goods from freight cars and cut firehoses to keep the cars burning. The crowd charged back. There was wild fighting and destruction.

Among the people drawn to the railroad yards by the sight of flames was Clarence Darrow. As he stood on the prairie watching the burning cars, he wrote later, he felt "sad to realize how little pressure man could stand before he reverted into the primitive."

Debs had repeatedly warned the strikers themselves to avoid violence and to stay away from the railroad yards.

He knew that any aggressive action or property damage would give the authorities the excuse they needed to smash the strike and destroy the union. Just as he feared, after the clash Debs and three other leaders were arrested for conspiring to obstruct the United States mails. They were released on bail, but rearrested a week later for violating the injunction which had been issued at the instigation of Olney. This time they refused to post bail and were imprisoned.

With their leaders gone and all further action prevented by federal troops and injunctions, the workers lost heart. The strike collapsed. Pullman reopened his factories, hiring only men who would sign pledges not to join any union. Six thousand former employees were refused jobs. The American Railway Union was destroyed and its members blacklisted. No railroad would employ them. Many changed their names and drifted to other parts of the country, looking for work.

In the meantime, Debs remained in prison, waiting for two events: the hearing for his violation of the antistrike injunction and the trial for conspiring against the United States mails. Neither of these charges was concerned with Debs as an individual; they were attacks against unionism.

As attorney for one of the railroad lines involved, Clarence Darrow was appointed to a joint committee of all the railroads to assist in breaking the strike soon after it started. He went to the town of Pullman and, upon investigating conditions there, decided that the men were right to strike. He refused to serve on the committee, explaining that his sympathies were with the workers, and offered to resign. His employers urged him to stay. They would remove him from the committee and trust him to remain neutral. Darrow agreed to remain, but as the strike grew more serious, his position grew more difficult and strained. When the antistrike injunction was issued, he was particularly disturbed. Here was a clear case of the government openly supporting one side against another in a dispute in which, he felt, the government should remain impartial. And when Debs was charged with conspiracy, Darrow reflected that, if anyone had conspired, it was Olney and the General Managers Association.

After the injunction was issued, Debs and several of Darrow's friends asked him to serve as attorney for the union leaders. Darrow knew it would be a long, troublesome case, taking all his time and paying nothing. It meant giving up a secure job for a highly uncertain future. In those days businessmen were unlikely to hire a lawyer who had defended a labor leader. And it was not as if Darrow were unhappy with his present employers and associates. Though he disagreed with many of their ideas, he respected and liked them as people, and was liked and respected in turn. He wished Debs had not asked for his help.

But Debs had asked, and when Darrow thought of the union members who had unhesitatingly endangered their own jobs in order to support the Pullman workers, he could find no excuse—"except my own selfish interest"—for refusing his assistance. The president of his company tried to dissuade him from resigning his job, promising a higher salary and offering to help with a political career. When he realized that Darrow was determined to aid the strikers, he announced confidently that the railroads would win, but that after they had done so, he would be glad to have Darrow handle some of the railroad's legal business again —about half of what Darrow had been doing at half his former salary. With this unusual arrangement agreed upon, they shook hands. Then Darrow walked out of the office of the Chicago and Northwestern Railroad and crossed to the side of labor.

Debs was brought to trial for conspiracy in January, 1895, before a judge who only a short time before had declared, "The growth of labor organizations must be checked by law." The spectators in the crowded courtroom leaned forward for their first look at the man portrayed by the newspapers as an infamous fire-eating agitator. They saw two men. One looked like a "well-groomed, successful corporation attorney"—"That's Darrow," whispered the onlookers. The other looked like a "disreputable social out-cast." The first man, with mild blue eyes and a benign expression, wearing a well-tailored suit with a starched, snowy white shirt and a flower in his buttonhole, was Debs. The second, carelessly dressed in a rumpled blue suit and wrinkled shirt, with unruly hair falling over his forehead, sprawling and slumping indolently far down in his chair, was Darrow.

At this trial Darrow used the techniques that were to become his hallmark. Instead of concentrating upon the fine points of law, he tried to create sympathy for Debs. He claimed that the real troublemakers were not his clients but those who had brought them into court. In almost every trial he was to single out one or two men, either on the prosecution staff or among the state's witnesses, and make them the targets of a blistering attack. And finally, he went beyond the immediate defense of the individuals he was representing, and used the trial as a public forum for explaining the social issues involved.

Through skillful questioning in a soft, mellow voice, he drew out the life story of Eugene Debs, showing him to be a man of integrity, high ideals, and selfless concern for the well-being of his fellow workers. This was followed by a denunciation of George Pullman as a ruthless exploiter of labor, a sham philanthropist who used his "model" town as an instrument of repression.

Debs had been charged with conspiring against the government by interfering with the United States mails and attempting to wreck the national economy by paralyzing the railroads. Darrow countered by accusing Pullman and the General Managers Association of conspiring to depress wages and of using the federal government to accomplish this purpose. If the railway managers had the right to organize, he argued, so did the workers. In a voice quite different from the one he used when questioning Debs, he boomed: "If the managers can organize to keep wages down, I can't understand why their workers can't band together to fight to raise their standard of living!"

Darrow subpoenaed George Pullman as a witness. He planned to question Pullman so that out of his own mouth the industrialist would reveal that the company had had twenty-nine million dollars in declared dividends and reserve funds, and yet had slashed wages below subsistence level. He also counted on the dramatic contrast between the mild-mannered Debs and the blustering Pullman. But Pullman could not be found. Darrow took advantage of Pullman's flight by contrasting it with Debs's courage.

Suddenly one of the jurors became ill and had to withdraw. The judge decided to postpone the case. Darrow, feeling that he had practically won and that a prolonged interruption and new trial would undo all his work, declared angrily: "The defense is willing to select a new juror and to have the transcript of the testimony read to him!" The judge refused and discharged the jury. Several jurors came down from the box, shook hands with Debs and his codefendants, and told Darrow they had been eleven to one for acquittal.

The case was never brought to trial again, and the government eventually dismissed the charges.

More serious was the injunction and its consequences to labor. Here, too, the main issue was labor's right to strike. The government claimed that, since strikes might injure an employer's property or business and cut down his profits, they could be banned by a court order to prevent such injury. In effect, the use of injunctions made it impossible for workers to strike.

One of the worst features of the injunction as an anti-union device was that it denied violators the right to a jury trial. A judge would simply hear evidence showing that the workers had continued to strike after an antistrike order had been issued. On this evidence he alone would decide if the workers were guilty of contempt of court and then pass sentence. Debs and the other union leaders were given six months in jail for continuing the strike in defiance of the order.

Darrow went to Washington to appeal the sentence before the United States Supreme Court. He argued that the injunction proceedings had denied Debs his right to a trial by jury. Furthermore, he said, if unions were legal, their members had the right to lay down their tools in an attempt to better their conditions. It was true that sometimes violence occurs during strikes: "Mankind," he said, "still retains many instincts of the brute, and at times of great public excitement or emergencies" these instincts take over. Nevertheless, he continued, though such violence is regrettable, it does not follow that strikes should be outlawed.

The Supreme Court praised Darrow's "earnest and eloquent appeal," but upheld the sentence and Debs remained in jail. This decision in the famous case, *In re Debs,* was one of the most important in the history of American labor. It sanctioned the use of the injunction as an antilabor weapon; it established the precedent of interfering with the rights of strikers in order to prevent interference with the rights of employers. It "strengthened the arm of arbitrary power," wrote Darrow, and made it possible for a man to be sent to prison without a jury trial.

Many people had been shocked by President Cleveland's open violation of states' rights; and not only labor sympathizers but conservative lawyers objected to "government by injunction." The dissenting voices became so loud that Cleveland appointed a federal commission to study the

Pullman strike. The commission denounced the Pullman Company and the General Managers Association; it exonerated the American Railway Union from the charge of violence. It urged compulsory arbitration and the recognition of labor organizations by employers. By the time the report was issued, however, the Supreme Court had upheld the injunction, and Debs was already in jail.

Four years after the strike, the Supreme Court of Illinois declared that the Pullman Company did not have the right to maintain a company town. Such a town "was opposed to good public policy and incompatible with the theory and spirit of our institutions." All property not actually used for manufacturing purposes had to be disposed of.

To the American labor movement the strike itself had been a major disaster, but this decision against company towns marked a tiny measure of progress. The workers did not want dubious "benefits" handed down from the Olympian heights of management. They wanted a fair return—a living wage—for their contribution to the industrial development of the country. It was an indispensable contribution, and so far they had received a disgracefully meager share of the wealth they helped to create. They wanted economic independence and justice, in accordance "with the theory and spirit of our institutions."

This was to be the great struggle of the next forty years. In it, Clarence Darrow, emerging from the Debs case as the defender of labor, was now deeply involved.

8

---◆---

At Forty

Darrow had expected his defense of Debs and his support of labor to harm his career as a lawyer. But when he resumed practice, there was no shortage of clients. True, most of them were poor and unable to pay high fees; many could pay nothing. To these Darrow not only gave his services without charge but often paid court and investigating costs out of his own pocket.

The Debs trial had given him a reputation as a defender of unpopular causes, a lawyer who would work as conscientiously for a poor client as for a rich one. His office grew crowded with the victims of social or industrial injustice. Workers who had been injured or maimed because of inadequate safety precautions or the widows of those killed in industrial accidents asked his help in getting compensation from employers. Harried union men appealed to him

76

for advice. The helpless innocents who had been cheated in one manner or another by the shrewd, unscrupulous operators prowling through the Chicago slums came to Darrow for the aid which he never failed to give. Many of his clients were Negroes. There was scarcely a white lawyer in Chicago at that time who would defend a Negro, but Darrow always said that he was color-blind. The color of a man's skin meant no more than the color of his eyes. Darrow felt, however, that since Negroes were singled out as victims of extra discrimination, they needed all the extra assistance he could give them.

Most of all came people who had been charged with crime, whose explanations of how they had come to commit the crime aroused Darrow's sympathies. When he first began to practice law, he had planned to handle only civil cases and wanted nothing to do with criminal law. He was an excellent negotiator, highly successful in settling cases out of court, a procedure that saved time and money for everyone concerned. Business litigation, not criminal trials, had been his main objective. In 1895 he became a member of a new firm, Collins, Goodrich, Darrow, and Vincent, whose specified purpose was corporation law. But when the anguished parents of a young boy charged with a crime begged him for help, or when the criminal himself came in distress, Darrow found himself unable to refuse. He had a quick imaginative sympathy that enabled him to get inside the troubles and feelings of others. His increasing understanding of *why* the crime had been committed led him to give his help, even in cases that seemed hopeless.

Though the firm prospered, the diverging interests of

Darrow and his partners made it impossible for them to continue together, and in 1897 Darrow set up his own firm. He continued to handle civil cases, and most of his income came from this source. But more and more of his practice was in criminal law.

His earlier views of it were changing: "Strange as it may seem, I grew to like to defend men and women charged with crime. It soon came to be something more than winning or losing a case. I sought to learn why one man goes one way and another takes an entirely different road. I became vitally interested in the causes of human conduct. This meant more than the quibbling with lawyers and juries, to get or keep money for a client so that I could take part of what I won or saved for him: I was dealing with life, with its hopes and fears, its aspirations and despairs."

As he worked with people accused of crime, Darrow began to probe into the social conditions that produced it. Altgeld's book had started him thinking about the nature of crime. Now he explored the broader aspects of human behavior. He studied anthropology and philosophy, learned as much about the physical structure of the human body as a medical student. He read novels, essays, and poetry— which he often quoted in courtroom speeches to illustrate his points—storing it all in his remarkable memory.

He enjoyed reading aloud. Guests at his home often found themselves spending the evening listening to Darrow read. Sometimes the reading would be interrupted by a brisk discussion of the ideas contained in the book. He loved to talk. When he was not talking in his own home, he was out at one of his numerous clubs or organizations, engaged in discussion or debate or giving a lecture. He spent one evening a week playing poker. His favorite physical diversion was bicycle riding.

Movement, action, change were essential to him. His energy seemed to increase as he grew older. The slow pace of a country law practice in Ashtabula had been stepped up to the ceaseless rush of Chicago. He was the first to come to his office at the beginning of the day, the last to leave it, and he left it only for another period of intense activity in another sphere. He often ate lunch—consisting perhaps of a piece of fruit—at his desk, using the time saved to read quickly through another book. There seemed no end to his curiosity or interests. He wanted to read everything, talk to everyone, go everywhere.

Jessie, however, felt very differently. She was never at home in the big city and longed for the simplicities of life in a small Ohio town. The new social theories that attracted Clarence, the political organizations, the literary clubs, the endless variety of ideas and people that made Chicago the source of new life and vitality for him meant nothing to her. She cared little for the friends Clarence was gathering around him, and, in turn, they did not take to her. Indifference turned to dislike and resentment, and soon Clarence found it pleasanter to meet his friends outside his home. When he did show up for dinner, he exhibited no appreciation for the meal Jessie had carefully prepared; he had little interest in food and hardly noticed what he was eating. It was the discussion that might take place over a dinner table that gave the dinner its significance. With

Jessie there was little discussion since, for the most part, she ignored the dramatic events which stirred her husband. The pretty, good-hearted young girl had turned into an unexciting woman, still good-hearted, but without the liveliness of either intellect or temperament to respond to the kind of man Clarence Darrow was becoming.

Clarence, in the meantime, was meeting other women—Chicago women, the "new women" of the period, who were fighting their way into the professions, who were bent on proving their intellectual and social equality with men. They were lively, intelligent, inquiring, resourceful. Darrow had never known such women before; he was strongly drawn to them—and they were equally drawn to him. He was no longer the inexperienced young boy who had courted pretty little Jessie Ohl; he was a self-assured man, with a warm and attractive manner that women found appealing. He inspired confidence. Progressive young women instinctively felt that in Clarence Darrow they would find a sympathetic response to their "new" ideas or actions. There would be none of the disapproval that generally greeted the attempts of women at the turn of the century to burst out of the confines of domesticity.

Clarence and Jessie drifted farther apart, and at last he came to feel that there was nothing left between them. After an unhappy period of indecision, he asked her for a divorce. He had no intention of marrying again, for he was now convinced that marriage seriously interfered with personal liberty.

Jessie was devastated, but she, too, realized that their marriage had indeed come to an end. "If you want to be free," she told him, "I won't put a feather in your way."

She went off to Europe with Paul, while Clarence arranged the divorce in an action that was completely free of contest or bitterness. When she returned, he provided a home and a generous allowance for her. Several years after the divorce, Jessie married an Ashtabula judge in whose court Darrow had appeared as a young lawyer.

He continued to see his son Paul frequently, taking him along on business trips and spending vacations with him. Paul remained deeply attached to both his parents. During a few of his summer vacations he worked in his father's office. Darrow never lost his temper with Paul. The only thing he insisted upon was that Paul get an education. When the boy wanted to leave school for good after graduating from high school, Darrow refused to permit this. He sent Paul off to Dartmouth with the agreement that his son try it until Christmas, after which he would be free to leave. Paul liked it and remained the full four years.

For a while after he left Jessie, Darrow kept having second thoughts. At the last formal meeting for the property settlement, he wept; and about a year later he went to see Jessie, telling her the divorce had been a mistake. But he finally began to appreciate his new bachelor existence. He was free to do as he liked, see whom he liked, keep whatever hours he pleased.

When he opened his own law office, Clarence had taken into the firm a young cousin of Jessie's, Francis S. Wilson. Some time after the divorce, Darrow and Wilson took rooms together at the Langdon Apartments, a new and unusual residence club. Each tenant had his own private apartment, but there was a common dining room and a common drawing room. The tenants were drawn from the most progressive and creative elements in the city: writers, artists, the social service workers centering around that remarkable institution, Hull House.

Hull House had been established less than ten years earlier in the middle of Chicago's worst slum by a group of socially conscious women headed by Jane Addams. They were determined to relieve the squalid living conditions of the city's industrial workers. It was Chicago's first settlement house, and the forthright ladies who volunteered their services were among the country's first real social workers and social scientists. In addition to helping poor families in the neighborhood of Hull House, they campaigned for safer working conditions, prohibition of child labor, free and compulsory education, and special juvenile courts. They were part of the great reform movement that sprang into existence to counteract the evils produced by industrialism.

In their cooperative dining room and parlor, the tenants of the Langdon Apartments entertained people as advanced and stimulating as themselves. Chicago was going through a social and cultural ferment that made it one of the most exciting cities in the world. Hull House had been established in 1889; the University of Chicago, richly endowed by the city's new millionaires, had opened its doors in 1892 with a roster of brilliant professors. A young journalist, Theodore Dreiser, had spent several years in the city, gathering impressions for the novels he was soon to write, and other talented young people from the small towns of the Midwest were beginning to congregate in the metropolis. The Art Institute, the Chicago Symphony Orchestra, the Newberry Library were already in operation. All this was reflected in the guest list at the Langdon Apartments.

It was an atmosphere in which Clarence Darrow thrived. It was, on the broadest scale, an extension of the talkfests in Amirus Darrow's little shop, to which young Clarence had listened so avidly. He and Wilson took two three-room flats and converted them into one spacious apartment where they entertained their many guests, when they were not down in the main parlor. Darrow soon became one of the most popular residents, leading discussions, reading aloud, joining in the singing and dancing. On his fortieth birthday the other tenants gave him a party—the best, said Clarence, he had ever attended.

His years at the Langdon Apartments were among the happiest in his life. He was still fairly young; he was free and unpressured and living in a milieu that nourished all his interests and abilities. He had a host of good friends, with new ones constantly being added. Two summer vacations were spent traveling in Europe. His practice was branching out into the new and absorbing fields of labor and criminal law, and he was beginning to participate in the political life of the city as well. At forty, he had at last found his place in the world.

9

The Right to Strike: The Kidd Case

Throughout the 1890's the question of labor's right to organize and strike continued to agitate the country. As factories grew larger and industry more powerful, the individual workingman had less to say about the conditions under which he lived and worked. If he was grossly underpaid or brutally overworked, there was nothing he could do about it. If he asked his employer for relief, he was told he was free to leave—there were a hundred unemployed men eager to replace him at even lower wages—or he was marked as a troublemaker and fired. The worker's only recourse was to join a union and hope that a large-scale strike would inconvenience the employer enough to make him agree to some slight increase in pay or a few improvements in working conditions.

The employers, on the other hand, from huge industrialists to small manufacturers, regarded a union as a conspiracy to cut down their rightful profits. Strikes interfered with business and production, and disturbed the smooth functioning of an industrial society. This view was vigorously upheld by the press, by government authorities, by the law itself which declared that a strike was a "criminal conspiracy" to injure business. The whole idea of unionism was regarded as a threat to individual enterprise.

Clarence Darrow, however, strongly dissented. In his view, the threat came not from unions, which tried to secure decent working conditions for their individual members, but from the law which put property rights above human rights. It was not the union organizers who were guilty of conspiracy but the big companies, who conspired against their employees, forcing them to work under intolerable conditions at substandard wages.

Darrow had expressed these views in his defense of Eugene Debs during the Pullman strike. A few years later Thomas I. Kidd of the Amalgamated Woodworkers' International Union was charged with criminal conspiracy for leading a strike, with the same legal questions involved as in the Debs case. Once again the right of workers to organize and to strike was being denied by the government, and once again Clarence Darrow hastened to uphold this right.

The strike was against a woodworking factory owned by George M. Paine of Oshkosh, Wisconsin. The average wage for a man employed by Paine was ninety-six cents for a ten-hour day; women received eighty cents, children sixty-five cents for the same working day. Though his company was operating at a good profit, Paine decided to increase his earnings by gradually firing the men and replacing them with women and children. Wisconsin law set fourteen as the minimum age for child factory workers, but Paine got around this by having fathers who were desperate for money sign false age affidavits for their children. Actually, many of these young workers were no older than ten.

Wisconsin law also required that workers be paid weekly, but Paine paid his employees only once a month, using the money for his own purposes in the meantime. There were other grievances. After the workers arrived in the morning, the factory doors were locked and no one was permitted to leave. Talking was frowned upon: "No unnecessary talking will be allowed during working hours," ran the rules, and "Loud talking or shouting cannot be allowed except in case of accident or fire." No one could leave his workbench for any purpose without special permission. In fact, no one could even quit his job without permission: "Employees who quit their places or the employ of this company without our consent or a reasonable notice of such intention, are subject to damages." The factory was run, as Darrow remarked during the trial, like the state penitentiary except that prisoners were at least fed and allowed to sleep on the premises and kept warm during the winter, whereas the Paine employees had to make do with miserable unheated slum tenements and broken-down shacks.

After a fourth of the men had been discharged, the woodworkers organized themselves into a union and sent a letter to Paine asking him to stop turning over the men's jobs to women and children, to pay wages weekly as required by law instead of monthly, to raise wages, and to recognize their union. Paine ignored the letter. He also refused to negotiate, first with a committee and then with individual employees who went to see him.

A strike was called under the leadership of Thomas Kidd. Paine kept his factory going with nonunion workers and tried to get an injunction forcing the strikers to return to work. The Oshkosh courts refused, saying that American workingmen had a right to leave their jobs. Paine's next move was more successful: he had the district attorney arrest Kidd and two other leaders on charges of conspiring to injure his business. Kidd sent for Darrow, and another "criminal conspiracy" trial of labor began.

The trial lasted three weeks. Darrow's summation at the end, lasting two full days during which he did not once refer to any notes, became one of the classics of labor history. William Dean Howells, editor of the *Atlantic Monthly,* called it "as interesting as a novel." This could be said about many of Darrow's courtroom speeches. He presented facts in a swiftly paced narrative manner, interspersed with ironic or philosophical comments, more in the style of a novelist than a lawyer. The Kidd summation was printed and distributed all over the world.

As he had done at the Debs trial, Darrow went beyond the immediate situation and used the trial to educate the public. He delivered an eloquent historical summary of man's long fight against oppression and tyranny. He presented the case not as a defense of three particular men, but as an "episode in the great battle for human liberty." At the same time, he appealed to the sympathies of the jury by giving a detailed and moving description of Paine's mistreatment of his employees. Finally, he put the case into its larger perspective by saying that finding the defendants guilty would do more than just send three men to prison, it would be saying to all American workers "that whatever the insult and the abuse and the outrage that is heaped upon them they must bear it in silence, or a jury will send them to jail."

Again as he had done in the Debs trial, he attacked the attackers, claiming that the real criminal was not Thomas Kidd but George Paine, who was using the legal machinery of Wisconsin for his own private and selfish purposes. The real conspirers were not the union leaders but Paine and the district attorney who had conspired together against the rights of workers. "There is a conspiracy, dark and damnable . . . one of the foulest conspiracies that ever disgraced a free nation."

He went beneath the surface issues to the real conflict: "Disguise it as you may . . . there is but one thing in this case, and that is the right of these men to organize for their own defense and to strike if they see fit. This is not a criminal case. It is an action brought by employers of labor to ruin and crush their men."

"I appeal to you," he concluded, "not for Thomas I. Kidd, but for the long line of despoiled and downtrodden people of the earth. . . . I know that you will render a verdict in this case which will be a milestone in the history of the world, and an inspiration and hope to the dumb, despairing millions whose fate is in your hands."

The jury responded to his appeal. After only fifty minutes of deliberation they voted "Not Guilty." Clarence Darrow had won another round for labor.

10

---◆---

Many Directions

There seemed no limit to Clarence Darrow's energy. All during the 1890's, as his law practice increased so did his participation in politics, labor problems, social and cultural activities, until he seemed to be juggling several careers at once.

There was, for example, his career in politics. It had begun in a small way back in Ohio, where he had been elected city solicitor of Ashtabula. In Chicago he became a campaign speaker for the Democratic party. His support of the Democrats had been strengthened by his admiration and friendship for John Altgeld, the party leader in Illinois. When Altgeld ran for reelection as governor in 1896, Darrow agreed to run for Congress at the same time.

Darrow attended the Democratic national convention of 1896 as one of the delegates for Illinois. The explosive issue of that convention was the free coinage of silver. It was the pivot around which all other issues clustered, the cause that split the country into hysterically warring factions.

Conservative economists, bankers, and big businessmen wanted to base American currency on gold, arguing that it provided stability. More radical economists, together with farmers, workers, and small tradesmen, wanted to base currency on silver. There was far more of it in the country than gold, which meant that more money could be put in circulation to keep pace with the commercial and industrial growth of the country. The supporters of gold wanted a strict limitation of the coinage of silver, in a fixed ratio to gold. The silverites, however, wanted its free and unlimited coinage, with the amount increasing as the country produced more goods.

"Free silver" became a fighting term and one of the most hotly debated issues the country has ever known. The "gold-bugs" insisted that only the gold-backed dollar was an "honest dollar," while the great mass of farmers and workers shouted that only free silver could express the true spirit of democracy. The silverites fought with the zealous fervor of men who have suffered grinding economic hardship. A popular slogan of silverite Kansas farmers declared: "Kansas had better stop raising corn and begin raising hell!"

Both Darrow and Altgeld were silverites. The Democratic convention, under Altgeld's leadership, came out for free silver. The next problem was whom to nominate for President. The question practically answered itself in one of the most astonishing oratorical displays ever heard in the United States.

Toward the end of the debate between the supporters of gold and the free silverites, a delegate made his way up to the platform. He was William Jennings Bryan, thirty-six years old, a former congressman from Nebraska. Audacious, energetic, and fantastically eloquent, Bryan had been working busily for two years, gathering support for silver—and for himself. He had carefully prepared the way for this moment.

At his opening words, the twenty thousand delegates in the swelteringly hot Chicago Coliseum fell silent. His impassioned but clear and bell-like voice moved his listeners as no one had ever been moved at a political convention. He touched every chord, religious, sentimental, idealistic, speaking not as a politician but as a humble citizen "clad in the armor of a righteous cause . . . the cause of humanity." He annihilated the gold supporters with his final lines: "You shall not press down upon the brow of labor this crown of thorns; you shall not crucify mankind upon a cross of gold!"

When Bryan finished his famous "Cross of Gold" speech, the audience broke into a frenzy of cheers, shouts, whistles, and tumultuous applause. Hats were thrown into the air, canes pounded on the floor. Among the few who remained calm and unimpressed were Darrow and Altgeld. The next day Altgeld said to Darrow, "I have been thinking over Bryan's speech. What did he say anyhow?" Altgeld wanted the convention to nominate "Silver Dick"

Bland of Missouri, but the delegates nominated, instead, the "Boy Orator of the Platte," as Bryan was called. As for the Illinois slate, Altgeld was nominated for governor, Darrow for congressman.

It was a wild and fanatic campaign with the Republicans convinced that, if Bryan and free silver should win, our national institutions would be destroyed, business crippled, and the peace and prosperity of the nation forever doomed. Mark Hanna, manager of the Republican campaign, spent enormous sums of money, eagerly contributed by banks, railroads, and big corporations, to defeat Bryan who had not one tenth the money behind him. Workingmen who wanted to vote for Bryan were threatened with loss of their jobs if they did so. In the end Republican William McKinley was elected.

Soon afterward, the production of gold was substantially increased. This automatically put more money in circulation, and the silver issue, which had almost torn the nation apart, faded quietly away.

Along with Bryan, Altgeld and Darrow were defeated, Darrow by only a hundred or so votes. He was relieved. "I did not want to be in political life," he wrote. "I realized what sacrifices of independence went with office-seeking." He was not, however, through with politics.

Bryan ran twice more for the Presidency and was defeated both times. Darrow campaigned for him the first time, not because he admired Bryan, but because he wanted to give the Philippines their independence. This was the campaign issue in 1900. Darrow told a mass meeting in Chicago that he did not want to give up "the republic of Jefferson" to gain "the empire of McKinley."

In 1908 Bryan wanted Darrow to campaign for him on the issue of guaranteeing bank deposits by the government. Darrow said his trouble was putting money into the bank, not getting it out. Bryan then suggested that Darrow speak on the election of senators by direct vote. Darrow replied that he did not care how senators were elected as long as we had them. Instead of making campaign speeches that year, Darrow took a vacation. He had had enough of Bryan.

But Darrow and Bryan were not finished with each other. They were to meet again almost twenty years later under circumstances as dramatic as those of the 1896 convention.

Other channels for Darrow's energy were writing and lecturing. He spoke for pleasure, seldom accepting a fee, even paying his own expenses when necessary. His subjects ranged far from the law. He talked on science, philosophy, and literature, on the social ideals of Tolstoy, the skepticism of Robert Ingersoll, the fatalism of Omar Khayyám.

At that time the work of Omar Khayyám was considered daring and Ingersoll was attacked as irreligious. But Darrow embraced unpopular literary figures just as he championed unpopular social causes. In 1899 he published a book, *A Persian Pearl and Other Essays,* in which he discussed not only the *Rubáiyát* of Omar Khayyám but, among other subjects, the work of Walt Whitman whose poetry was frowned upon as unconventional and shocking

—a view that in no way deterred Darrow from writing about him.

In the spring of that same year he gave a lecture on Omar Khayyám at the White City Club in Chicago. After it was over some friends—John H. Gregg, the inventor of the Gregg shorthand system, and his wife—introduced him to a young woman they had brought to the lecture. Ruby Hamerstrom was a journalist working on the Chicago *Evening Post*. She was twenty-six, Darrow forty-two. He was instantly attracted by her vivacious manner. He invited her to dinner. She refused. He talked to her until the lights of the hall were put out and then held on to her hand so that she could not leave. At last she pulled herself free and left without yielding to his insistence that she agree to see him again.

Darrow sent messages to her through the Greggs, but there was no response. He asked the Greggs to arrange a meeting, but nothing happened. He began to suspect that Mrs. Gregg was not giving his messages to Ruby.

The reason for Ruby's reluctance was not that she did not care for him. On the contrary, she said later, she fell in love with him at their very first meeting, just as he had with her. But she was engaged to a New York stockbroker and felt it would be best—or at least safest—not to see Darrow again. However, when she heard that he was blaming innocent Mrs. Gregg for their failure to meet, she discussed the situation with her fiancé who was at the moment in Chicago. He felt there would be no harm in Ruby's having just one dinner date with Darrow in order to explain her position and exonerate Mrs. Gregg. So she let

Darrow know that she would accept his invitation if Mrs. Gregg were included. She was taking no chances on being alone with him.

At dinner Darrow announced that he was lecturing that evening and asked Ruby to come along. She refused, saying she was spending the night with Mrs. Gregg and would go home with her right after dinner. She could not stay up late for the lecture anyway because she had to be up early the next morning.

Darrow teased her out of these transparent excuses with such charm that at last she gave in. As soon as they dropped Mrs. Gregg at her home, Darrow turned to Ruby and told her he had never met anyone he liked so much, adding that it was only fair to warn her that he had been married once and never intended to marry again.

Ruby replied: "That's fine, because I'm getting married myself."

He refused to take her engagement seriously, saying they would find some way of breaking it. "People who like each other as much as we do shouldn't be separated."

Ruby laughed—but she broke her engagement, leaving a clear field for Darrow.

The year 1900 was a busy, profitable, and generally happy one for Darrow. He saw a good deal of Ruby Hamerstrom, whose quick, well-informed intelligence and colorful personality delighted him more and more.

In that same year William Randolph Hearst, on his way to becoming head of the largest string of newspapers in the country, added the Chicago *Evening American* to the papers he already owned in San Francisco and New York. He hired Darrow to incorporate the *Evening American* and later, in 1902, the *Examiner,* and asked him to continue as general counsel for the Chicago branch of the Hearst journalistic empire. This organization, together with two or three other larger corporations for whom Darrow did legal work, paid so well that he could more easily accept cases from clients who could pay little or nothing.

The connection with the Hearst newspapers had another advantage besides money. It provided an outlet for Darrow's writing ambitions. He often said that he would much rather have been a writer than a lawyer. His essays and stories now appeared in the Chicago *Evening American.* Most of the stories were based on his legal experience. In the series called "Easy Lessons in Law," he used his own cases to illustrate legal and economic injustices. Their presentation of harsh facts made them part of the new realistic literature just beginning to appear in America. The essays were generally on the same literary and philosophical topics as his lectures. He received no money for any of these pieces, but their appearance was immensely gratifying to their author's soul.

Another development during this period was Darrow's law partnership with John Altgeld. Altgeld had suffered greatly since 1896. His deep chagrin at not being reelected governor had been compounded by serious illness and the loss of his personal fortune. He had put almost all his money into constructing one of the most ambitious of the early skyscrapers, a sixteen-story building called the Unity Block, completed in 1891. In the depression years following the panic of 1893, many of his tenants had gone out of business and closed their offices or were unable to pay their rent and were carried free by their sympathetic landlord. Of the prosperous tenants, many had moved out after Altgeld pardoned the Haymarket anarchists. He could not meet his interest payments and the banks, hostile to him ever since the pardon, refused to extend any more loans. By 1899 all the mortgages were foreclosed, and the Unity Block, which Altgeld considered his greatest personal achievement, was lost.

Everything seemed lost. His fortune, his health, his political career, certainly his hope and confidence were gone. He was in his early fifties but felt he was too old to begin a new career or return to the practice of law. He told Darrow "he would be content to crawl under a sidewalk and die."

In an attempt to rouse him out of his apathy, Darrow and several other friends persuaded Altgeld to run for mayor in 1899. He refused to appear on the Democratic ticket because he felt the party, which had slipped out of his control, was betraying the interests of the common people. He agreed to run as an independent.

The big fight in local Chicago politics at the turn of the century was over streetcar franchises, a fight in which Darrow took a leading part. As Chicago spread out, more public utilities of every kind were needed. These were run, at a substantial profit, by private companies licensed by the city. All the desirable licenses or franchises, especially those granting the right to operate streetcars, were a rich source of graft to dishonest members of the city council.

They awarded the franchises to whoever paid them the highest bribes.

The most successful briber was Charles T. Yerkes, a buccaneering traction magnate who had come from Philadelphia, where he had served a jail sentence for embezzlement, to the greener pastures of Chicago. Here, with the help of dishonest aldermen, he seized control of the major streetcar lines and proceeded to amass a huge fortune. To increase his earnings, he also began building the elevated lines that would circle around the downtown business section, giving it the name of the Loop. He charged maximum fares for minimum service and safety. When the afflicted straphangers on his dangerously overcrowded cars tried to protest, there was no one to listen because the appropriate city officials had been bought off by Yerkes. At the same time he cheated the city treasury out of thousands of dollars by paying only a fraction of the amount the franchises should have brought. He was the most unscrupulous, the most brazen, the most skillful, and the most slippery business-political manipulator in a city filled with experts of the same kind. Theodore Dreiser, one of the first writers to describe the unprincipled power operations of the new age, made Yerkes, under the name of Frank Cowperwood, the central figure of three novels: *The Financier, The Titan,* and *The Stoic.* Another social commentator said Yerkes was "like a plague that had stricken the city."

The 1899 elections took place just before Yerkes' franchises came up for renewal. He asked for an extension of fifty years. Altgeld and Darrow wanted public ownership of the trolley lines. Altgeld was one of the few men Yerkes had been unable to bribe. When Altgeld was governor of Illinois, the state legislature had passed by a large majority a number of bills that would have made possible an "eternal monopoly" for Yerkes, and without any payment on his part to the city of Chicago. Yerkes offered Altgeld a tremendous bribe, reputed to be half a million dollars, not to veto the measures. Altgeld vehemently rejected the money, though with it he could have saved his beloved Unity Block and shored up his collapsing fortunes; he was already facing bankruptcy. He wrote a veto message "that fairly scorched the rails of the line." When Yerkes heard of the refusal to accept the bribe, he said: "I admire that man!"

It was to make certain that Yerkes did not strengthen his hold on the streetcar lines that Altgeld agreed to run for mayor. He and Darrow addressed large crowds every night. The crowds were really coming to cheer Altgeld, who still had a loyal following. But the principle for which he was fighting, city ownership of public utilities, was too new. The voters were not ready for it, and Altgeld lost the election.

However, the campaign had brought him back into the public eye, and political leaders once more began to respect his influence. He was invited to speak all over the country and to take an active part in the forthcoming Presidential convention.

Altgeld now felt ready to return to the practice of law, and Darrow urged him to become his partner. Altgeld feared he would be of little use, but Darrow overcame his doubts and made him the senior member of the firm of

Altgeld, Darrow and Thompson. In a short time Altgeld began to display his early legal brilliance and contributed his
full share to the work of the firm.

He continued to make speeches, generally before political
and labor groups and in defense of his favorite causes.
In the spring of 1902 he went to Joliet, about forty miles
from Chicago, to address a protest meeting against England's war with the Boers in South Africa. Darrow and
Altgeld felt that England's actions were unjustified. With
their customary sympathy for anything small against anything big, both men were holding meetings to arouse support for the small Boer nation.

When Altgeld finished speaking, he felt dizzy. He tried
to leave the stage, but collapsed and had to be carried to his
hotel. At midnight Clarence Darrow was summoned from
Chicago, but by the time he arrived, Altgeld was dead.

Darrow, deeply grieved, brought him back to Chicago
and arranged the funeral. He asked two clergymen to
speak, but both found pretexts for refusing. Cautious people were still wary of associating themselves in any way
with John "Pardon" Altgeld. The funeral addresses were
made by Darrow himself and by Jane Addams, founder of
Hull House. The pioneering women of Hull House, through
their volunteer work for Chicago's unfortunates, had
carried out Altgeld's own convictions about the responsibility of helping the poor and weak. As governor, he
had responded to their pleas for social legislation; the
first workable factory law in Illinois was passed during his
administration. It prohibited child labor, set an eight-hour
day for women, and created factory inspectors. He had

appointed a member of Hull House as the first woman inspector in the state and placed another on the state board of charities. He had done everything in his power to secure protection and equal rights for women. Like Darrow, he had been a favored guest at Hull House, and it was eminently fitting that Jane Addams should say farewell.

Altgeld, Darrow, and Jane Addams had all shared the same vision, had all, as Darrow said of Altgeld, "placed the love of man above the love of self." They were full "of kindness, of charity, of infinite pity to the outcast and the weak," but they were also fighters who expressed their convictions in practical action. They accepted reality: instead of dreaming of perfection, they did what was possible to improve an imperfect world. Darrow had found in Altgeld not only a warm friend and respected political leader but a rare idealist whose inspiration and encouragement Darrow was never to find again.

11

Settlement Without War

It was partly to carry on the work of Altgeld that Darrow consented to run for the state legislature in 1902. Chicago's streetcar problems were still unsettled, but now the voters were closer to accepting the idea of public ownership. Shortly after Altgeld lost the election of 1899, Yerkes had organized the Union Traction Company and transferred to it all his property and franchises. He then used his phenomenal powers of salesmanship to sell it at a grossly inflated price and, after pocketing fifteen million dollars in cash, waved an airy good-bye to the city he had fleeced and moved on to the fresh opportunities of New York.

The Union Traction Company gave no better service to the public than Yerkes had. Streetcars were more crowded than ever, they seldom ran on schedule, and double fares were charged at transfer points. The citizens of Chicago became so indignant that early in 1902 they insisted that a referendum be held on the question of city ownership of street railways. Leading the drive was the Public Ownership League, of which Clarence Darrow was the chairman of the executive committee. The vote was overwhelmingly in favor of the city's taking over all public transportation.

Now it was necessary to elect a legislature that would carry out the expressed wish of the public. The Municipal Voters' League asked Darrow to become the candidate from his district. His first impulse was to refuse. It would interfere seriously with his law practice and throw him directly into the "dickering and trading, anxiety and trouble" of political office which he disliked. But since there was no one else to take Altgeld's place in the battle against civic corruption, he agreed to run.

He had always been on friendly terms with the Democratic party leaders of his own local district and had helped in many campaigns. He assumed they would automatically put him on their ticket once he had consented to run, especially since the Democrats had just come out with a strong reform platform advocating public ownership of utilities. To his surprise, they rejected him as a candidate, explaining that his name had become "anathema to Chicago businessmen." Darrow promptly announced that he would run as an independent and conduct his own campaign.

His campaign was completely unorthodox. He told the voters that he did not want the office, that he was running only to safeguard municipal ownership of street railways, which was as much their fight as his, and that if elected he would not get any jobs or do any special favors for his constituents.

In the middle of the campaign two things happened that gave Darrow more publicity than the Democratic party machine could possibly have provided if it had been behind him. The first was a dispute between the Union Traction Company and its employees, the streetcar workers, who wanted more pay and the right to organize their own union. To avoid a disrupting strike, both sides agreed to arbitration by a three-man board. Darrow was selected as the workers' representative, which increased the esteem in which he was already held by labor groups in Chicago.

The second was another arbitration case, one that put his name into national newspaper headlines. In the spring of that year more than a hundred and fifty thousand anthracite mine workers had gone on strike against low wages, long hours, and poor working conditions. They also wanted recognition of their union, the United Mine Workers. The entire industry was shut down. John Mitchell, the young president of the UMW, regarded strikes only as a last resort and asked for arbitration, but the owners refused. As the winter approached, the public, whose sympathies were with the mine workers, began to fear a coal shortage. President Theodore Roosevelt was asked to intervene, but it was only when he threatened to seize the mines that the owners agreed to arbitrate. A commission was appointed to hear the facts and arrive at a settlement. Clarence Darrow was named chief attorney to present the union's side of the case.

Several days after this appointment was made public, the Chicago elections were held. Darrow received more votes than the combined totals of the other candidates. Immediately after the election, the settlement of the streetcar dispute was announced: Darrow had gained a large pay increase for the workers plus other benefits. Enthusiasm for Darrow mounted higher than ever; there was talk of organizing a union labor party and running him for mayor in the spring election.

Darrow himself was too busy to think about his political future. For the next three months he was away in Scranton and Philadelphia at the anthracite mine hearings. He worked with prodigious energy, spending as much as fifteen hours a day taking part in the sessions, questioning witnesses, visiting the coal mines, investigating every detail of the miners' lives, and preparing his case. The seven-man commission appointed by President Roosevelt received a complete picture of what it meant to be an anthracite miner: how much the miners earned; how many hours and under what conditions they worked; how much they had to spend on food, clothing, rent, education, and medicine; in short, how it really felt to be a miner under prevailing conditions.

The mine operators were represented by George F. Baer, president of one of the companies involved. Before the hearings began, Baer had said: "The rights and interests of the laboring men will be protected and cared for, not by the labor agitators, but by the Christian men to whom God in His infinite wisdom has given control of the property interests of the country."

Darrow's ideas about the rights of workingmen were

very different, as he made clear in a final summation lasting eight hours. Unlike Baer, who read his closing speech,
Darrow spoke without referring to a single note or docu-
ment. When a young associate tried to give him the accu-
mulated mass of notes, Darrow brushed him aside. It was all
there in his memory.

The courtroom could not hold the crowds who wanted to
attend; among those who did get in were journalists whose
reports were printed all over the world. From time to time,
as Darrow spoke, the audience broke into spontaneous applause. Sometimes there were outbursts of laughter at his
humorous sallies.

A newspaperman said later that the address summarized
all the "hopes and pleas" of trade unionists everywhere.
Darrow spoke for the right of workers to organize in an
attempt to improve the wretched conditions under which
they were forced to work. He presented specific evidence of
these conditions. There were the low wages, with nearly
half the miners earning less than two hundred dollars a
year out of which they had to buy tools and blasting pow-
der. There were the long hours: mine firemen had to work
twelve hours a day, seven full days a week throughout the
year, shoveling up to fifty tons of coal a day. The work was
dangerous, causing a high percentage of crippling accidents
and deaths with no compensation from the companies. He
described the work of little boys who inhaled the destruc-
tive anthracite dust while they worked for fifty-eight cents
a day.

At this point Darrow angrily asked the assembled company owners and their battery of lawyers: "Where are

your sons and your daughters? Let me say this, that until you, Mr. Railroad President, or you, Mr. Lawyer, will take your child by the hand and sit him down to pick at that trough of moving coal, until you will take your pale girl to the silk mills, let *me* speak for the children of the poor."

He did not rest his case on facts and figures alone. His unique courtroom talent lay in his ability to express legal arguments in terms of real people in real distress. And he was less concerned with immediate technical guilt than with underlying causes, which again he presented in human terms. Thus he argued that the real blame, the moral responsibility for the strike lay with the mine owners who "refused to recognize their workmen as human beings."

He took the practices of the mine owners and showed how they affected not impersonal labor units, but living people. One of the coal companies hired only men who would live in company houses, which were leased on a day-to-day basis "at the will and pleasure" of the mine owner. If any worker displeased him—by joining a union, for example—he could then say it was his "will and pleasure" that the miner vacate his house immediately. Before he agreed to take part in the arbitration proceedings, this owner fired a group of men who had been active in the strike and evicted them from their homes. Darrow gave a harrowing description of these evictions, which had taken place in a driving rain and with scarcely any notice.

The wife of one of the miners and his mother—a hundred years old and blind—were both sick in bed. When the sheriff arrived with the eviction notice, the miner asked for two hours in which to find a place to move the sick women.

The sheriff passed this request on to the mine owner who curtly refused. "Not ten minutes," he said, and sent his own superintendent along to see that the evictions were carried out promptly. "And they dumped them out into the middle of the street," said Darrow. "They took out their stoves and their chairs and their beds . . . and they left them in the street. And they got through with this glorious job at six o'clock at night of a November day, when the rain was coming down and it was dark, and they were there upon the street—men, women, children; the well, the sick, the blind, the infirm, the helpless, two miles from any shelter. And then the superintendent turned his back upon them and drove away and went home and got his supper."

If the employers, argued Darrow, had the right to use such weapons as evictions from company houses, unwarranted firing of workers, blacklisting which prevented a man from getting work in other mines, and the use of armed troops against defenseless miners and their families (which had been done in the anthracite region), then workers had an equal right to their weapons of union organization and strikes, even if they sometimes caused violence. "Gentlemen," said Darrow addressing the assembled mine owners, "this was an industrial war. You on your side were fighting 147,000 men with their wives and their children, and the weapons you used were hunger and want . . . the most cruel, deadly weapon that any oppressor has ever used to bring men to his terms."

He declared, as he had in the Pullman and Kidd cases, that this was more than an isolated strike. It was part of labor's long struggle to relieve "the darkness of their lives." It was "one of the most important contests that has marked the progress of human liberty since the world began."

When Darrow finished, his listeners broke into sustained applause for five minutes. The proceedings had to be temporarily halted while people crowded around to shake his hand and congratulate him.

A wage increase with several million dollars in back pay was awarded the miners, plus a shorter work day and other benefits. A plan for future working conditions was drawn up; it brought industrial peace to the anthracite region for the next twenty-five years. Perhaps best of all, the principle of arbitrating labor disputes was successfully used. Darrow had long urged this method of conducting industrial relations. It had now been put into practice with his own eloquent assistance.

12

---·◆·---

Assemblyman Darrow

When Darrow came back to Chicago, he was hailed as a beloved champion of labor. Thousands gathered at a meeting to hear him describe the events of the anthracite hearings. The draft-Darrow-for-mayor movement grew stronger. While he was still attending the hearings, friends and political associates had gone to Pennsylvania to urge him to run for the office. A Union Labor party was formed, and Darrow was invited to be its nominee on a platform of public ownership of utilities. It was also suggested that he run on the regular Democratic ticket: the old Altgeld forces within the party wanted him, while the opposition group were afraid he might win if they ran someone else against him.

Darrow delayed his answer, hurrying off to Springfield to take his seat in the state legislature, which had already been in session for several weeks. The question, however, persisted: Would he run for mayor? Party leaders and newspapermen kept after him for a definite answer.

He sought the advice of politically experienced friends and labor leaders, such as Samuel Gompers, president of the American Federation of Labor, and John Mitchell, president of the United Mine Workers. At last he did what he had wanted to do all along: he announced that he would not run. A mayor was an executive; he had to enforce the laws, however bad they were. The important thing, Darrow felt, was to have good laws. He decided he could be of greater value in the legislature where the laws were made. As mayor, handicapped by existing laws, there was little he could do about public ownership of utilities; as a member of the state legislature he could fight for a bill permitting cities to own and run their utilities and to raise money for this purpose.

Darrow expected to be of more use making the laws than carrying them out. But he quickly learned that the state legislature was as inefficient—"more time is fooled away at great expense"—and as bogged down in political maneuvering as the city administration: "I soon discovered that no independent man who fights for what he thinks is right can succeed in legislation. He can kill bad bills by a vigorous fight and publicity, but he can get nothing passed."

One law that he could not get passed was a state law regulating labor injunctions. Ever since the Pullman strike he had led the movement against "government by injunction." In 1900 he had gone to Washington as chief witness for a bill to prohibit the use of injunctions in labor disputes involving interstate commerce. He urged that injunctions should be abolished altogether or should not be issued where an act was already prohibited by an existing state or federal law, or that violators of injunctions should at least be granted a jury trial. But the congressional committee before which he appeared was unsympathetic to his views, and the bill failed to pass. He had hoped to put through a similar state bill, but though he worked strenuously, it, too, was unsuccessful.

Among the bad bills he fought to kill were those deliberately proposed to invite bribes for corrupt members of the legislature. A bill to impose heavy taxes on big corporations would be offered; the big corporations would pay several members handsome sums of money to vote against the bill, and the bill (which was never intended to pass in the first place) would die. Many of the members thought Darrow, as an outspoken antagonist of monopoly, would naïvely support such bills taxing the big companies, but he was too shrewd and experienced not to detect their real purpose. He voted against them and urged corporation owners to refuse payment of "tribute" money.

Another group of bills that he successfully helped to defeat were those naming new offenses as crimes or increasing penalties for violating existing laws. Darrow thought there were altogether too many laws already, and that lawmakers were always thinking up new things to punish. Many of these laws were such vague catchalls that a court could imprison people guilty of the most trivial misdeeds. "No wonder that crime increases in America when men sit up nights contriving new accusations for sentencing others to jail."

Some of the people who wanted to add new laws were reformers. Although Darrow often found himself working with professional reform associations against the regular political groups, especially on such matters as public ownership of utilities or child labor, he did not like the reformers of his day. He felt they were too often intolerant, fanatical, and meddlesome, and interfered with individual liberty. They were always asking for new laws to prohibit some form of human activity: drinking, gambling, Sunday entertainments, the small "enjoyments of the poor."

He objected to their methods as well as their aims. There was a hardness about them; their attempts to regulate personal conduct—which they had no right to do in the first place—were done in a "small, pestiferous, nagging manner that makes life a burden." They confounded "sin with pleasure; they think the world should be gloomy and sad, and pleasure should be postponed till kingdom come." Darrow felt that life was painful enough without the puritanical restrictions of the reformers. He was all for joy, for taking whatever relaxing and pleasant escapes life could afford—the theater, dancing, drinking, card playing. To him the real sin was the prohibition of joy.

His work in the legislature was not all negative, however. He put through one bill of his own and helped pass others. His own bill raised the amount of compensation for deaths caused by negligence from five to ten thousand dollars. Its intention was to help the families of workers killed in industrial accidents. Darrow could be a shrewd political manipulator himself when necessary. He deliberately proposed the bill in what he knew was an extreme and unacceptable form, and then dickered with its opponents till he effected a "compromise," bringing it down to the form in which he had originally planned it. It was passed almost unanimously.

He also helped put through an improved child labor law, continuing the advance in this field begun by Governor Altgeld at the instigation of the Hull House ladies. Another law that he helped formulate and get passed permitted prisoners to manufacture certain products in jail. The trade unions strongly opposed this, considering prisoners' work unfair competition, and were surprised and even displeased by Darrow's support of the bill. He explained that he considered it inhuman to keep prisoners idle, locked in their cells all day long. Since he refused to support or oppose a bill for any reason except the merits of the bill itself, he went ahead with it despite the unions.

His major effort was for the bill permitting public ownership of utilities. This was a long, complicated battle, with Darrow as the untiring leader of the public-ownership forces. He marshaled votes, foiled the delaying tactics of the bill's enemies, and skillfully fenced with hecklers on the floor of the legislature. He was exceptionally good at political infighting, thinking quickly and speaking to good effect. He was good at another kind of fighting, too. During one heated discussion the supporters and the opponents of the bill came to blows. Darrow knocked his adversary down and jammed a wastebasket over his head. In the end, the opposition retired in defeat, and the bill was passed.

This bill did not automatically establish public ownership of utilities. It simply gave cities the right to own and run their utilities if they wanted to. Now there followed a much longer and infinitely more complicated attempt to get the Chicago city administration to take advantage of the new law. It lasted almost four years, with Darrow in the middle of a whole series of confusions and difficulties.

In 1904 a new city administration was elected, with a mayor who was for city ownership of streetcars. One of his first acts was to appoint Clarence Darrow as special corporation counsel in "absolute charge of all traction litigation."

But the actual process of taking over the trolley lines by the city stumbled along, hampered by opposition within the administration and by the mayor's own lack of decisiveness. Darrow tried to plow his way through the morass of opposition and apathy, then gave up and resigned. He said that nothing could be achieved through politicians, whose one interest was "to make a living out of politics." The mayor persuaded Darrow to withdraw his resignation by promising definite action at last. But the mayor's good intentions were thwarted by his lack of skill as a political leader. More complications followed, more delays, more disagreements between Darrow, the mayor, the city council.

In the end the mayor was defeated for reelection, and the plans for city ownership came to nothing. But the long effort and the loud protests of the public had its effect: no private company ever again dared behave as Yerkes had. Service on the trolley lines was greatly improved, and the city received a substantial payment for the use of its streets by private traction companies. The flagrantly open bribery of public officials came to an end.

His experience as an active lawmaker strengthened Darrow's belief that good government could be provided only by electing men "who have convictions and who are in politics to carry out their convictions." Altgeld had been such a man. Darrow himself was another.

13

---◆---

New Partners

Springfield, the capital of Illinois, is two hundred miles from Chicago, a considerable distance before the day of airplane travel. Darrow found the journey too inconvenient by train, so on days when the legislature was not in session he remained in Springfield, catching up on his reading. He enjoyed the reading, but he was distracted by thoughts of his neglected law practice back in Chicago. He discovered that it was almost impossible to attend to the affairs of the legislature and to his profession at the same time. To make matters worse, his firm, which had been reduced one third by the death of Altgeld, was now cut down another third when his remaining partner left to take care of family property. A new partner was plainly needed.

On the same floor of the building in which the firm of Altgeld, Darrow and Thompson had their offices was the

office of another lawyer, Edgar Lee Masters. Masters' chief
interest was poetry, and he would later become famous for
his *Spoon River Anthology,* cast in a series of ironic epi-
taphs attacking the narrow-minded bigotry of a Midwestern
village. In 1903, however, he had not yet made his reputation as a poet. He was known more for his articles on
politics and constitutional law than for his volumes of poetry, and he had to earn his living as a lawyer.

Altgeld had known his father, and whenever he and
Masters met in the hallway onto which their offices opened,
they would stop and talk. There had also been a few earlier
legal contacts between the two men and between Masters
and Darrow.

In the spring of 1903, at the end of the legislative session, Darrow invited Masters to join his firm. Masters hesitated. His highly conventional wife disliked Darrow; his
stiffly conservative father-in-law strongly disapproved of
Darrow's ideas. Masters, however, was already thirty-four
years old, "getting nowhere," and had fallen out with his
law partner. His income was uncertain and, at best, inadequate. Darrow's firm was one of the most eminent and
successful in Chicago. The offer was too good to refuse, and
Masters finally accepted it, hoping to earn and save enough
money so that after a few years he could devote all his time
to writing poetry.

The partnership lasted for eight years and, on the face of
it, seemed to make sense. Masters, highly logical and well-
organized, ran the office and prepared cases. Darrow, who
excelled at dealing with people, made court appearances,
handled the direct contacts with clients, and brought in

most of the new business. Masters had a cold, forbidding manner that chilled clients and juries, so this division of the firm's labor worked out well.

But Masters remained one of the few people who, knowing Darrow, disliked him. Though he recognized Darrow's "amiable qualities," and even found pleasant "his drawl and his sleepy ways, his humorous turns of speech, his twisted ironies," he did not quite believe that his generosity and goodness were sincere. Masters was a tense, unhappy man, who seemed to resent Darrow's easy, lounging, "old-fashioned" soul. He felt there was a similarity between Abraham Lincoln and Darrow, saying "he was more like Lincoln than anyone I had ever known." But Masters, who disliked Lincoln and later wrote a book attacking him, did not intend this as a compliment. He felt the two men shared a kind of shrewdness and cunning, and that their apparent simplicity of manner was nothing but the result of acting ability. Others, however, took up the comparison and used it as a form of high praise for Darrow, seeing in him the Lincolnesque qualities of compassion and humanity.

While Darrow was away in Springfield, his law practice fell off sharply. He had no regrets, considering his political education well worth the sacrifice. As soon as he returned to Chicago, clients came flocking back, and the firm prospered more than ever. He made Francis Wilson, with whom he was still sharing an apartment, a partner. The firm was now Darrow, Masters and Wilson.

One of Masters' complaints was that Darrow was forever

going off on some non-legal venture like lecturing or debating, leaving Masters behind to do the work. On one occasion when Darrow was due at court, a telegram came at the last minute saying he was delayed in Cincinnati where he had lectured the night before. Masters had to take his place before the jury and lost the case. Masters also complained that Darrow never turned any part of his lecture fees into the firm's treasury. According to Darrow, there were no fees.

Right after he returned from Springfield, Darrow was plunged into another injunction embroilment. This was in connection with the Kellogg strike, one of the most violent ever seen in Chicago. There were almost daily riots, with fights between pickets and scabs. Injunctions were issued, jail sentences and fines were imposed, but still the trouble continued. Darrow, representing the strikers, protested against the injunctions, declaring that if every union man were jailed, he would continue the picketing himself.

On the very worst day, early in July, 1903, a thousand strikers gathered and threw stones at the Kellogg factory, smashing hundreds of windows. It was inevitable that the strikers should again be arrested and should again have to appear in court with their lawyer.

But where was their lawyer? He had completely vanished. It was later discovered that on that same morning he had married Ruby Hamerstrom. There was a champagne breakfast at the home of the Greggs, who had introduced them four years earlier, and then Darrow and his bride slipped away on the train to Montreal. From there they sailed for Europe where they traveled about for almost three months, leaving the harassed Edgar Lee Masters to defend the union.

Masters fought the injunctions strenuously, attending court every day, working late almost every night throughout the hot summer. But the opposition was too strong, the antiunion bias of judge and public too great. Almost thirty years would have to pass before the federal government would recognize the right of workers to organize and to strike, and would devise an anti-injunction law to protect these rights from arbitrary government interference.

Darrow's friends were unprepared for his sudden marriage. They knew he had been paying special attention to Ruby Hamerstrom, but ever since his divorce some six years earlier, he had persistently criticized the limitations of marriage. He argued that in many cases it provided no "opportunity for individual development" and that "from the nature of things a large percentage of marriages must bring more pain than pleasure." Who would have thought that Darrow would get married again? And to someone like Ruby. She was strong-willed; she could outtalk even Darrow himself; she was possessive in her fierce devotion to him. Nevertheless, here was Darrow behaving like any inexperienced young swain with no thought of the possible consequences.

And how, his friends went on to ask, could Darrow, of all people, leave abruptly in the middle of a labor crisis, and for such a purely personal reason? Did he feel that Masters could carry on, or was he convinced that it was impossible to fight the injunctions successfully at this time?

These questions remained unanswered. Darrow was gone.

If he felt any remorse for his actions, he did not allow it to interfere with the pleasures of his honeymoon. He had a glorious time in Europe. The turbulence of strikes and injunctions, the vexations of the state legislature, the pressures of a busy law practice melted away while he and Ruby traveled through France and Switzerland, Holland, Germany, England. The only work he did was the writing of a nostalgic book of boyhood reminiscences called *Farmington*. It was a thinly disguised autobiography; the names of people and places were fictional, but the events, the emotions, the later reflections were those of Darrow's own life seen through a gently idealized haze. It was one of his best-written and best-selling books.

When they returned, the Darrows lived briefly in his old rooms at the Langdon Apartments until Ruby could find an apartment of their own, which she proceeded to turn into a proper setting for her husband. One of the reasons for the failure of Darrow's first marriage was Jessie's reluctance to entertain his friends, her inability to create the kind of social atmosphere in which he flourished. Ruby was exactly the opposite. She felt as much at home in an active social world as Darrow; she could hold her own in any discussion. She could listen to Darrow read aloud to his friends—his favorite form of entertainment—and respond to what she heard with wit and intelligence.

She was a skilled hostess. Gone were the days of Darrow's informal bachelor beefsteak-and-potato meals for his friends. Ruby served formal dinners, from caviar to liqueurs. Darrow was not an easy man to feed: there were not many foods that he liked, and his dislikes were expressed with vehemence. "I don't like spinach," he once said, "and I'm glad I don't, because if I liked it I'd eat it, and I'd just hate it."

Ruby did more than take care of him at home; she managed every detail when they traveled. Darrow moved around a good deal in connection with his law practice and on lecturing and debating trips. Ruby did all the packing, made all the transportation and hotel arrangements, and handled the engagement schedules.

They quarreled a good deal and made no attempt to keep it private. He often warned friends in her presence to beware of getting trapped by marriage. But the quarreling did not cut very deeply. It was more like the spirited exercise of two mettlesome individualists who were too accustomed to argument and debate to be distressed by it; indeed, it is possible that they often enjoyed disputation for its own sake. Darrow would probably have become bored with a meek, acquiescent wife. He enjoyed people who spoke up, who expressed their true feelings and opinions no matter what the results might be.

Darrow became increasingly dependent upon Ruby; the time would come when he would go nowhere unless accompanied by her. She in her turn devoted herself exclusively to the care and defense of Clarence Darrow.

The next few years passed with the same busy rush. Darrow's prodigious energy continued to spread itself over the fields of law, politics, debating, lecturing, traveling, writing. He even taught a course on court procedure at the Illinois College of Law.

In the summer of 1904 he attended the Democratic national convention in St. Louis, where he spoke for the small group of Altgeld Democrats still remaining in the party. The only Presidential nominee this group could find who would support the Altgeld reforms was William Randolph Hearst, for whom Darrow was working in the double capacity of lawyer and political adviser. Darrow nominated him halfheartedly, then used the rest of his speech to urge the party to return to the ideals of Jefferson and Altgeld. His candidate was rejected, and Darrow, losing interest, withdrew from the convention and spent the next few days visiting the St. Louis Fair with his son Paul. Before the next party convention, Hearst asked Darrow if he should try to run for office again. Darrow said No, which was not what Hearst wanted to hear. He decided to run and asked Darrow to support him. Darrow said No again and was fired.

Darrow had never been a party man in the usual sense. Party loyalty for its own sake seemed unintelligent and even dishonest; he believed the only honesty lay in following one's own convictions, wherever they led. While still an active Democrat, he had once campaigned for a Republican whom he believed better qualified than the Democratic candidate for the office. And he warmly admired Eugene Debs who, after the failure of the Pullman strike, had been attracted to socialism and eventually became the Presidential nominee of the newly formed Socialist party. Darrow never agreed with Debs's political ideas, but that did not prevent him from extending his friendship to a man whose gentleness and courage he respected. He had been a Democrat as long as the party supported Altgeld's ideals. When it became just another routine machine party, Darrow retired from an active role in its affairs.

From St. Louis, Darrow and Ruby went to Estes Park, Colorado, for the rest of the summer. Here Darrow wrote *An Eye for an Eye,* a sociological novel about a worker living in the slums who is led by his desperate and brutalized life to commit a murder. Darrow used the novel to express his views on poverty and crime. Like his short stories it anticipated the documentary novels of the 1930's, dealing with the miseries of the poor and with society's harsh treatment of its own victims.

Back in Chicago, Darrow devoted himself to getting his son started on a career. Paul had just graduated from Dartmouth, where he had gone at his father's urging. He tried several business jobs and finally went to work in a new bank. Darrow had invested in it heavily and persuaded Masters to invest five thousand dollars. For several months the bank did well, but then Paul discovered that the officers were planning some illegal deals. He told his father, who immediately went to the Chicago clearinghouse and arranged to pay off the depositors and close the bank. Darrow and Paul took over the tellers' windows and distributed the piles of cash. Almost everyone, including the stockholders, got all or part of their money back, except

Darrow and Masters, both of whom lost virtually all their savings.

A few years later Paul again joined his father in a business venture, this time with more success. Darrow and several of his friends bought some patents which included an option on a gas plant in Colorado. Paul moved there and spent the next twenty years managing the plant, selling it in 1928 at a substantial profit. Just before going to Colorado, Paul married a girl who worked for his father's law firm; in due time Darrow became the pleased grandfather of three little girls.

14

---◆---

Ordeal in Idaho

In December, 1905, Frank Steunenberg, former governor of Idaho, opened the gate to his home. In doing so, he touched off a mechanism that exploded a bomb. It tore him to pieces and ignited another ferocious battle in the war between labor unions and mine owners. Clarence Darrow was to be drawn into the thick of this battle.

The hard-metal miners of the West were organized into a union called the Western Federation of Miners. It was very different from its Eastern counterpart, the United Mine Workers, whom Darrow had represented in the anthracite coal hearings. The UMW was a businesslike group concerned chiefly with raising wages and improving working conditions. They tried to secure these ends as peacefully as possible. Their leader was John Mitchell, a calm, quiet, conservative young man who always sought arbitration and disapproved of strikes except as a last resort.

The Western Federation was a fighting, revolutionary union whose hatred of employers had become as great as the desire for better wages or fewer hours. The Western hard-metal mining region of Idaho, Colorado, Utah, Montana, and Arizona was still open frontier country, and the miners were still rugged individualists, quick to take offense at any interference with their rights or liberties. One of their leaders was Big Bill Haywood, a large, violent man of almost legendary physical strength, a giant "son of the Rockies." He had fought and scratched his way up, as he himself put it, "from the bowels of the earth," through sufferings that had left him with a deep core of vengeful, primitive, yet oddly idealistic passion.

He represented, in exaggerated form, many of the miners who burned with the same sense of injustice. There was good reason for their emotion, however extreme their expression of it may have been. The powerful owners of the Western metal mines had shown themselves callously indifferent to the welfare of the men and their families, and had done everything to prevent organized action by the miners.

The mines were dangerous places in which to work and few safety precautions were taken. The twelve-hour day, the seven-day week were common. Wages were disgracefully low and were issued, not in real money, but in company scrip which could be used only at company stores charging inflated prices.

The worst period began in 1892 when the mine owners

of the Coeur d'Alene area in Idaho announced a wage cut of a dollar a day. When the miners refused to work, strikebreakers were brought in. Fights broke out between strikers and scabs. Armed Pinkerton guards were hired by the mine owners. A guard killed a striker, whereupon the strikers armed themselves, attacked the guards, and drove out the strikebreakers. The state militia was called but felt itself incapable of dealing with the embattled miners. The governor appealed to the President, who sent in federal troops. With Coeur d'Alene under martial law, the mine owners were able to bring back the strikebreakers.

The failure of their strike would have been hard enough for the miners to bear, but the general in charge of the federal troops was not finished. He erected a bullpen in which he imprisoned hundreds of those who had taken part in the strike and discharged all local officials who had shown any sympathy for the strikers, replacing them with his own men.

Mine workers throughout the West were so incensed by the treatment of the Coeur d'Alene strikers that in the following year, 1893, they organized the Western Federation of Miners, one of the most militant unions in the country. They would meet force with force, they declared, violence with violence. From then on a series of turbulent outbreaks took place in the mining regions. The worst were the strikes at Cripple Creek, Leadville, and Telluride in Colorado, and at mines throughout Idaho but particularly around Coeur d'Alene.

Every strike became a small war, with guards and deputy sheriffs equipped with machine guns and even armed cavalry lined up against armed strikers. Mines were dynamited; men were shot. The local communities were terrorized, with soldiers breaking into private homes and men being seized on the streets at the slightest suspicion.

Whenever the miners lost a strike, the same routine was followed: bullpens were set up in which strikers and sympathizers, even women and children, were imprisoned. When writs of habeas corpus were issued, soldiers refused to obey the judges' orders to produce the prisoners. On one occasion, when the highhanded actions of the military leader had been upheld by the Colorado State Supreme Court, the union's lawyer said the Constitution was being violated. He was told by the judge: "To hell with the Constitution; we're not following the Constitution!"

Along with this went the firing of sympathetic local officials and the blacklisting of workers so they could never find employment in other mines. Union leaders were "deported" by being forcibly carried over the border into another state and warned never to return, even though they left families and homes behind them. Storekeepers were ordered not to sell anything to union men, and relief supplies sent by other unions were confiscated by the soldiers.

It was open war. Federal troops patrolled the mining areas. Resentment and hatred grew. Miners flocked in larger numbers to the Western Federation, which grew strong enough to make itself felt in politics. In Idaho it supported Frank Steunenberg, throwing enough votes his way to elect him. Steunenberg had been a member of the printers' union and understood the labor viewpoint. Now, thought Federation members, unions will get a fair deal in Idaho.

But in 1899, during another big strike in Coeur d'Alene, Governor Steunenberg intervened on the side of the mine owners. He called in federal troops who again established martial law and imprisoned more than a thousand miners in a crude barbed-wire enclosure, keeping them there for months under appalling conditions. The governor also instituted the hated "permit" system which made it impossible for members of the Western Federation to get jobs in Idaho. To the mine workers, Steunenberg became another object of hatred, a traitor who had delivered them to their enemies.

After his term as governor expired, Steunenberg became a sheep rancher and banker, living quietly and prosperously in Caldwell, Idaho. But the miners had never forgotten how he betrayed them. When the bomb exploded and the question of who could have wanted to kill him arose, there were many who replied, the Western Federation of Miners.

There was a great outcry over the murder, and large rewards were offered for finding the killer. All strangers in town were closely investigated. When the hotel room of one of these was searched, a piece of the fishline and some of the plaster of Paris that had been used in setting the bomb were discovered. The man was also found to be going under a false name. He was better known as Harry Orchard, though this turned out not to be his real name either.

As soon as Orchard was arrested, the newspapers charged that he was the tool of the Western Federation of

Miners and that the union was the real criminal. But Orchard refused to speak, and nothing could be proved. After ten days of his silence the authorities decided to place a famous private detective, James McParland, in charge of the investigation.

McParland was the manager of the Denver branch of the Pinkerton Detective Agency, which at that time specialized in labor troubles. It provided a variety of services to industrialists and to employer groups like the Mine Owners' Association in their fight against unions. It supplied strikebreakers, labor spies, and armed guards. The word "Pinkerton" itself was enough to make a workingman shudder or swear. McParland was one of the ablest and shrewdest of the Pinkerton detectives. He had established his reputation for counterunion activity thirty years earlier in the Pennsylvania coal fields.

First he had Orchard thrown into solitary confinement in a dark cell, as part of a softening-up process. After ten days of this, Orchard was brought to see McParland who talked to him about the Bible and the hereafter, about sin and repentance, and the "awful consequences of a man dying in his sins." Day after day, for thirty days, McParland carried on a one-man revival meeting, appealing to Orchard's religious fears. He assured him that where a conspiracy to murder existed, the man who had done the actual killing was not as guilty as the instigators of the deed. It was made clear to Orchard that the only way to save his own life was to accuse someone else of having hired him to commit the murder.

Finally, at the end of thirty emotion-filled days, Orchard,

with tears running down his cheeks, made a full confession. He admitted the murder of Steunenberg. He went on to admit twenty-five other murders and a host of lesser crimes. Above all, he said that he had been hired to do away with Steunenberg by the leaders of the Western Federation: Charles Moyer, the president, Big Bill Haywood, the secretary-treasurer, and two prominent union figures, George Pettibone and Jack Simpkins. Another union member, Steve Adams, was named as having helped plan the details of the killing. As soon as he confessed, Orchard was removed from the penitentiary to a small house nearby. He was given good food, new clothes, reading matter, and small sums of money to buy additional comforts. Important state officials came to visit him, and *McClure's Magazine* bought the story of his life.

In the meantime Idaho officials went to Denver, where the Western Federation had its headquarters, with extradition requests for the men named by Orchard. Technically the men were not subject to extradition since they were not fugitives from Idaho, but Colorado officials were happy to cooperate, and Moyer, Haywood, and Pettibone were arrested. Simpkins had disappeared and was never found. The other three were put in jail and forbidden to get in touch with anyone, not even a lawyer. They were denied their constitutional right of habeas corpus, the right of every man to a public hearing where he must be told the reason for his arrest. Before daybreak next morning they were whisked away to the railroad station and put on a special train which sped on cleared rails across Utah and

Wyoming into Idaho, where they were imprisoned in the penitentiary at Boise.

The whole procedure was, of course, highly illegal. The Federation lawyers protested against this outright kidnapping, and the case was carried to the United States Supreme Court. The Court declared that though "the fundamental rights of the men had been violated in Colorado," they were now held by a competent court in Idaho which could properly charge and try them.

There was nothing the Federation could do now except arrange for their defense. They sent for Clarence Darrow.

Idaho authorities knew that Orchard's confession alone was not enough to convict the Federation leaders of having conspired to murder Steunenberg. A corroborating witness was needed, and the only man to fill this role was Steve Adams, who had been named by Orchard as having worked with him in planning this and other crimes. Adams was living on a homestead in Oregon, and again Idaho officials used highhanded methods to bring him into their jurisdiction.

He was arrested in Oregon on the charge of having murdered Steunenberg. He was denied a lawyer and, with no formal hearing, put on a train which took him directly to Boise. Here he, too, was put into the penitentiary and allowed to see no one except Orchard, who went to work to convince him that he would be hanged as a murderer unless he agreed to back up Orchard's story. After five days McParland came and added his urgings, assuring Adams that if he signed an acceptable confession he would be set free. McParland also brought along his Bible from which he read selections appropriate to the occasion.

After several days Adams, faced with a choice of hanging or going free, confessed as instructed by McParland. Now he, like Orchard, was removed from a cell and put into a comfortable private cottage. His family was brought from Oregon to stay with him.

No one working for the defense was permitted to see him. Darrow finally got around this by persuading an uncle of Adams to convey Darrow's offer to defend Adams if he repudiated his confession. Adams promptly did so. The state just as promptly pressed another charge against him. He was accused of having murdered a claim-jumper in northern Idaho several years earlier.

By this time Haywood, Moyer, and Pettibone had been in jail for more than a year. Almost two years had passed since Orchard had confessed to the killing of Steunenberg. Yet the state dropped everything and proceeded without delay to try Steve Adams for the murder of an unknown claim-jumper whose death the state had ignored until now.

The action shifted three hundred miles to the north, to Wallace, Idaho, in the county where the claim-jumper was alleged to have been killed and where the trial would be held. Defendant, lawyers, prosecutors, reporters, and the ever-present McParland all moved up to Wallace for the curtain raiser to the main act, which was, of course, the case against the Western Federation leaders.

The trial began in February, 1907, and lasted three weeks. Early in March, Darrow made his summation to the jury. He brushed aside the question of Adams' guilt or innocence and came directly to the heart of the matter. The trial, he said bluntly, "is a fraud from beginning to end." It was nothing but a bald attempt to get Adams "back into their hands," so that the state could again threaten him with hanging unless he agreed to support Orchard's story, laying the blame for the Steunenberg murder on the Western Federation of Miners. "They are after bigger game," he cried. This was not, of course, news to any judge or lawyer involved in or observing the Idaho trials. What was news was Darrow's open discussion of this maneuver in court, his refusal to fight the case on any ground but the real issue.

The jury was unable to reach a verdict. After two days they were split seven to five for acquittal. The judge dismissed them and held Adams for retrial. This was considered a victory for the defense, since Adams could not under the circumstances be a state's witness in the trial against Haywood, which was to come next.

Leaving Adams in the jail at Wallace, the lawyers, prosecutors, newspapermen, and the rest of the assemblage trooped back to Boise for the headline event. On their heels came an influx of labor leaders, mine owners, political observers, journalists. Even William Jennings Bryan came along to watch, expressing his sympathy with the defense.

Boise was hostile to Darrow, identifying him with the unpopular cause he was defending, but he was used to this kind of animosity. With his gift for attracting friends even in the most antagonistic environment, he found a few with whom he could relax. In fact, he liked Boise and admired its natural setting. He was glad to return to it from Wallace, where he had suffered from the rain and the intense cold.

Everyone went into high gear. The prosecution, deprived of a star witness, tried to build up Orchard as a reformed character whose unsupported word could be accepted. In a highly irregular attempt to gain public sympathy for him, the governor permitted pre-trial newspaper interviews of Orchard. The confession itself was printed in *McClure's Magazine*.

This was a tremendous boon to Darrow who, until then, had been severely handicapped in preparing his defense since he knew nothing of the state's case. Now he quickly organized a small army of investigators and sent them out to track down every detail of the confession. When the case came to trial, he was able to call almost a hundred witnesses to disprove many of Orchard's statements. Some of these witnesses were able to answer the question many people had been asking: If Orchard was not acting for the Western Federation of Miners, what motive did he have for killing Steunenberg?

Darrow's investigators found that, in 1899, Orchard had been one of the miners forced to leave during the Coeur d'Alene strike when Governor Steunenberg had called in federal troops. Earlier, Orchard and a few others had discovered what was to become the Hercules mine, one of the richest deposits ever found and ultimately worth millions of dollars. When he fled, Orchard had had to sell his one-tenth interest for practically nothing. Several of

Darrow's witnesses claimed that Orchard had threatened Steunenberg's life in revenge for his loss.

By the time the trial began, the entire country had taken sides. Eugene Debs, crying "Arise, ye Slaves!" wanted to lead an army of workingmen into Idaho to free Haywood, Moyer, and Pettibone, who had been in jail some eighteen months. President Theodore Roosevelt, on the other hand, called the prisoners "undesirable citizens," whereupon tens of thousands of workers and sympathizers began wearing large buttons which read, "I Am an Undesirable Citizen." There were parades and demonstrations of workers throughout the United States. Two hundred and fifty thousand dollars was contributed by labor to the defense fund.

The trial opened in May, 1907, with every seat in the courtroom filled and crowds standing outside straining to hear the proceedings through the open windows. It took almost a month to impanel a jury. Darrow's address to the jury began on July 24 and lasted eleven hours. He spoke, as usual, without notes, pacing back and forth in the tiny area reserved for the main actors in the packed courtroom. It was extremely hot, and Darrow had taken off his jacket, revealing suspenders into which he tucked his thumbs as he spoke. These "galluses" and his habit of pulling on them with his thumbs were to became famous. He was over six feet tall, with unusually broad shoulders, a deep chest and, commented one of the reporters, a "face like a crag."

Another reporter pointed out the paradox of Darrow, a man who hated violence of any kind, defending Haywood who did not hesitate to use violence against his enemies. It was true that Darrow did not like Haywood and disapproved of his methods, though he admitted they were sometimes unavoidable. In this instance, however, he believed that Haywood was innocent; furthermore, it was not Haywood but the Western Federation of Miners and its right to exist that he was really defending. As he said in his summation, "Mr. Haywood is not my greatest concern."

Darrow's speech, which many listeners considered the finest he had ever made, "a masterpiece of logic and emotional appeal," had two main themes. It presented the cause of union labor against the background of the great mine strikes, and it revealed Orchard as a man who could not be believed. With the removal of Steve Adams from the case, the state's entire argument depended on Orchard. If he were discredited, the state's case would collapse.

Darrow went over Orchard's record item by item. In addition to some twenty-five murders, Orchard had also dynamited mines, stolen ore, committed arson (including burning down his own factory to get the insurance), abandoned his wife and infant daughter without a penny, run off with a friend's wife and then deserted her to marry another woman bigamously. He had been a thief, a poisoner, a perjurer, and a kidnapper. Can you, Darrow asked the jury, convict a man on the testimony of someone like "Harry Orchard, an unspeakable scoundrel; Harry Orchard, a perjured villain; Harry Orchard, bigamist and murderer and coward; Harry Orchard, shifting the burdens of his sins upon these men to save his life? If you men can kill my client on his testimony, then peace be with you."

Toward the end Darrow was so tired that his voice

dropped to a whisper. He made a final plea for the cause of the worker, a plea that struck even unsympathetic listeners with its eloquence and sincerity. He reminded the jury, as he had reminded other juries, that he was not speaking just for the immediate defendant: "I speak for the poor, for the weak, for the weary, for that long line of men, who, in darkness and despair, have borne the labors of the human race."

When he finished there were tears in his eyes, and in the eyes of many others in the courtroom.

The jury retired at about ten that night. Some of the lawyers went home to bed, but Darrow could not sleep. He spent the whole night walking restlessly through the town.

At seven in the morning the jury reached a verdict: not guilty. The empty streets suddenly filled with people who greeted the news, just as the rest of the country was to do, with angry disappointment or wild rejoicing.

The prosecution was so upset by the verdict that it could not decide what to do next. Darrow arranged to go back to Chicago until the state could let him know what its next step would be.

Darrow, exhausted by the Haywood trial, had hoped for time to rest, but after only a few days in Chicago he was called back to Idaho. The state had decided to try Steve Adams again, hoping to use him as a witness in the next major trial, that of Pettibone.

As soon as he reached Boise, Darrow came down with influenza and a few days later developed a painful infection in his ear. He felt unable to go on with the Adams trial and asked to have it delayed, but the prosecution refused.

In the middle of the night Darrow's suffering became unbearable. He sent for Boise's only ear specialist who said that something serious, though as yet undetermined, was developing and that Darrow must be prepared to go to California or back to Chicago for an operation. It was out of the question for him to attend the trial. But how, asked Darrow, could he refuse to defend Steve Adams? Adams had rejected the state's offer of freedom and put himself into this dangerous position largely because of Darrow's promise to defend him.

When the doctor realized that Darrow's sense of responsibility for Adams would not let him rest, he reluctantly made arrangements for treatment during the trip to northern Idaho, where the trial was to be held. He lanced the ear and showed Ruby how to keep it drained and irrigated and how to give Darrow the injections of codeine he would need in order to endure the pain. All the way north, Ruby took care of the ear, sterilizing the equipment in the dining car or over a coal stove during stops.

The state had not wanted to risk a second trial in Wallace, which was friendly to Darrow. The new trial was to be held, instead, in the tiny town of Rathdrum, near the Washington border, not far from Spokane. There was no hospital in Rathdrum, so the Darrows went directly to Spokane to consult a specialist. He repeated what the doctor in Boise had said: something, possibly mastoiditis, was developing; the condition was extremely dangerous and might even be fatal; Darrow would be risking his life if he went on with the trial. Darrow felt that Steve Adams was also risking his life; he, Darrow, could do no less with his own.

The Darrows returned to Rathdrum, where they remained for two agonizing months. There was never a moment when Darrow was not in pain. Every night, all night long, Ruby refilled hot-water bottles which muted the pain enough so that he could sleep.

The second trial of Steve Adams was an almost exact repetition of the first. This time the jury voted ten to two for acquittal, and Adams was once more returned to jail, still unavailable as a witness for the state.

Immediately after the trial the Darrows went first to Portland and then to San Francisco, seeking relief for the infected ear. Again the baffled specialists shook their heads and advised continued watchfulness for whatever was developing. When Darrow received a telegram calling him back to Boise for Pettibone's trial, the San Francisco specialist warned him not to go, saying it might be fatal. Pettibone, however, wired that it might be fatal for *him* if Darrow did not return. Over the protests of Ruby and the doctor, Darrow wearily got back on a train. For two long days and nights, a trip that Darrow felt would never end, Ruby heated water and sterilized equipment in the dining car, treated his ear, and gave him injections of codeine. When they reached Boise, he went straight to the hospital.

By this time Darrow and everything that happened to him was news. Newspapers and magazines all over the country were following the trials closely and running special articles on him. A typical piece was "Who Is This Man Darrow?" in *Current Literature,* which said it was evident that Darrow was more than the usual hired attorney—"he pleads for a cause as well as for a client." It called him a brilliant speaker, quick of retort, incisive, epigrammatic.

Word of Darrow's serious illness spread through the newspaper world. While Darrow was in the hospital, a reporter for a Chicago paper came into his room and showed him a telegram which said: "Darrow reported dying. Interview him." Darrow said he was not ready for such an interview because he had not yet picked out his "famous last words," but would get right to work thinking of some.

When Pettibone's trial opened, Darrow's doctor was still uncertain of the cause or treatment of the infection. All he was sure of was that if Darrow went into court he might die. Darrow replied that he felt so miserable he did not care whether he lived or died, so he might as well go on with the case.

The Pettibone trial covered the same ground as the Haywood trial, with one important exception. At the first trial one of the other defense lawyers had cross-examined Orchard; he had shouted at the witness, abusing and antagonizing him. Orchard, used to such tactics, remained calm and unruffled, and did not change a word of his original statement. Now Darrow did the cross-examining, using a quiet approach. He did not go over the grim facts in Orchard's confession but tried, through his questions, to reveal the essential nature of the man himself. He asked Orchard to describe the way he had played on the floor with a friend's child, a child he was planning to kidnap; he asked how he felt about the friends whom he plotted to kill or betray, how he felt about the victims who had died in the buildings he had bombed. "As I went along," said Darrow later, "one could see the jury drawing from him in horror and disgust."

When he finished the cross-examination, Darrow was on the point of collapse and asked the court to end the session for that day. The next morning he was brought into court in a wheelchair. He could not stand. Speaking in a voice so low that the jury had to lean forward to hear, he explained that he was unable to go on. He gave a brief outline of what the defense would try to prove and promised that his associates would continue the case.

His associates, however, decided not to add anything to what Darrow had already done. They announced to the court that they would rest their case, offering neither evidence nor argument. This surprising move proved successful: the jury brought in a verdict of not guilty. Shortly afterward, Idaho dropped the case against Moyer, the third defendant. As for Steve Adams, he was extradited to Colorado where he was tried on still another charge, acquitted, and finally released.

Only Orchard remained. He was sentenced to death, but the sentence was commuted to life imprisonment. The rest of his life—almost fifty years—was spent in the penitentiary at Boise, where he received favored treatment.

After Darrow had been carried out of the courtroom, the next problem was how to keep him alive during the sixty-hour train ride to Los Angeles. The doctor thought he had little chance of surviving. Darrow said later that his sheer will to live kept him going: "I had been living for a long time and had formed the habit."

Somehow Ruby got Darrow to the hospital in Los Angeles. After a week of observation and tests, the doctors knew no more than they had before. They began to suspect that it might be nothing but badly overstrained nerves. All they could do was to advise rest and patience. Darrow left the hospital and moved to a small apartment nearby, where the doctors could keep close check on his condition. But when, after several weeks, there were no further developments, Darrow decided he might just as well be miserable back home in Chicago, where Edgar Lee Masters had been carrying on alone all these months. The doctors agreed. Tickets were bought and Pullman arrangements made. Just as he was about to leave, Darrow felt an odd sensation in back of his ear. The entire area had suddenly begun to swell. He was rushed back to the hospital, and the next morning an operation revealed a freak case of mastoiditis.

The operation was a success, but Darrow's general physical condition was so poor by then that it was weeks before he could leave the hospital and return to Chicago. He had been gone twenty-six months.

15

---◆---

Interlude

The long nightmare of pain and anguish seemed to be over. Darrow was no longer on the point of death from a mysterious disease. He was no longer under the harrowing pressures of doing battle with the state of Idaho. As his strength slowly came back, Darrow returned to the relatively simple problems of everyday life.

If his major life-and-death troubles were over, his minor ones were definitely not. For years Darrow had wanted to retire from law and concentrate on writing. Underneath the highly successful attorney was a frustrated author. He loved to write and sincerely thought he could be of more use to the world spreading his ideas on the printed page than in the courtroom. To him the ideal life would be spent writing, lecturing, traveling. The money for this would come, he hoped, from his savings and investments. But

Darrow, shrewd and practical in law and politics, was doomed to failure in the field of finance. He had lost ten thousand dollars, his entire savings, in the bank venture, and another substantial sum in another equally poor investment.

His next attempt was an investment in the Black Mountain gold mine in Mexico. This promised excellent returns. Whenever Darrow felt low or irked by the vexations of trial practice, he would comfort himself with the thought that some day he would retire and live on the income provided by the mine. In 1907, however, a serious business depression made it necessary to reduce his holdings. But the point at which his stocks should have been sold came just after his mastoid operation, when Darrow was precariously balanced between life and death. Frantic telegrams arrived from his partner in the mine, urging him to sign the papers authorizing the sale of their stocks. Ruby refused to disturb Darrow. The doctors said that any strain might kill him. Convinced that she was faced with the choice of saving either Darrow or their money, Ruby decided to let the money go.

Darrow was enraged when he discovered later what had happened. Again he had lost his savings; again his retirement had to be deferred.

When he took stock of his finances, he found that he had not only lost money; he was also deeply in debt. The Western Federation of Miners had spent so much money on the trials and had so little left that Darrow agreed to take a much lower fee than had originally been offered. This was more than swallowed up by the expenses of his illness—

doctors' bills, hospital charges, train journeys. It took him more than a year to pay these off.

His law practice had suffered during his absence and also because of the depression of 1907. New business had to be brought in. Darrow, now fifty years old and exhausted from the illness and difficulties of the past two years, no longer had the energy or the will to work as he had in the past. Instead of fighting cases through the courts, he turned increasingly to out-of-court settlements. He was able to effect compromises and agreements in disputes between private contestants, business organizations, workers and employers. His reputation for making such settlements grew, and soon he was regularly called upon as an impartial arbitrator by both sides in case after case, especially those involving labor.

Gradually, corporations and organizations of every kind asked him to serve as their regular lawyer. Even William Randolph Hearst came back to the fold. The mayor offered him his old job as corporation counsel for Chicago. Darrow refused, but accepted instead the job of special counsel for the city's traction affairs. He paid off his debts and once more settled into an active, profitable law practice.

When they had first left for Boise, Ruby had given up their apartment, putting the furniture in storage. On their return from California, she found a nine-room apartment on the top floor of a building on the Midway, near the University of Chicago. There were magnificent views of Lake Michigan and Jackson Park, as well as of the university. The rooms were large and beautifully proportioned, flooded with sunlight and air.

Darrow loved the new apartment. It was to be his home for the rest of his life. He had the walls between the three front rooms removed, making one huge L-shaped room, which he lined with bookshelves to house his constantly growing library. Here he entertained his friends, including many professors from the nearby university. He knew an amazing number of people. It was said that it took hours for Darrow to walk even the shortest distance in Chicago because he stopped so often to talk to persons he knew. His natural charm, his beguiling manner, his warm responsiveness, as well as his gift for conversation, drew others to him wherever he went.

His large front room also became the regular weekly meeting place of the Biology Club, whose members gave lectures and conducted discussions on scientific subjects. Darrow's interest in the natural and social sciences had persisted since his student days, and the knowledge he was now absorbing would prove excellent preparation for one of his most famous trials.

Life was once again smooth and pleasant. And then, in 1911, it all came to an end. He was asked to defend some labor leaders against a criminal charge, which appeared to be still another attempt to smash the growing power of the unions. But it was to be much more than another incident in the cause to which Darrow had given so much of his life. This would be his last big labor case. It would bring his career as the defender of labor to a shattering end. It would almost end Clarence Darrow himself.

16

---◆---

The McNamaras

The cataclysm that was to hurl Clarence Darrow out of the labor world took place in Los Angeles. It arose over the question of the closed shop. A closed shop meant that an employer would agree to hire only union men. Darrow approved of this principle and had written about it in a famous pamphlet, *The Open Shop*. He knew all the shortcomings of the closed shop, how unions could abuse it by fixing unreasonable terms of membership. But he felt that without it unions could not exist: "The open shop means only an open door through which to turn the union man out and bring the non-union man in to take his place."

Darrow had no illusions about labor unions or their leaders. They were like any other group of men: they could be wrong, unwise, unjust, even corrupt. In his pamphlet he said: "No one claims that all trade unions are wise or even honest, much less that they have not made endless mistakes in the past and will not continue to err."

Unlike many labor sympathizers, Darrow did not believe that the great mass of people were instinctively wise or good. Nor did he regard big businessmen as incarnations of evil and more innately selfish than workingmen. "I have known many men on both sides," he wrote in his autobiography, "but cannot say that any are better or worse than the others."

He was perfectly aware that trade unions were not ideal institutions, but they were necessary ones. In *The Open Shop* he said that the mission of unionism "is to protect the weak against the strong. In the great industrial strife that has come down through the ages, trade unionism has fought the battles of the workman." Darrow supported unions with all his skill and devotion because he was convinced that workers had never received what they were entitled to; but "when they get more than they ought to, I will probably be against them."

It was his hope that the time would come when workers and employers would stop fighting each other and realize that their interests would be served best by peaceful cooperation. "Then all men will be brothers, and the highest good of all will be the fond desire of each." Darrow knew, of course, that this was a Utopian dream, but he did want to see some easing of industrial tension in his own lifetime.

One of the most notorious open-shop cities in the United States was Los Angeles. Its big businessmen and industrialists were fiercely determined to keep unions out of the city. At their head was General Harrison Gray Otis, publisher of the Los Angeles *Times,* an aggressive, dictatorial, ultraconservative man with a special hatred of unions, though in his own youth he had belonged to the printers' union. He used every means, however ruthless, to fight them. It had become a personal crusade; he went out of his way to stir up labor antagonism, filling the columns of his paper with vituperative abuse of union organizers. He expected open warfare with unions to break out, and in anticipation had mounted a small cannon on his car. He was called "the generalissimo of the open-shop forces in Los Angeles."

He organized the Merchants' and Manufacturers' Association, whose primary purpose was to fight unionism, and made it so powerful that every employer of labor was forced to join. As a result, it became almost impossible for a union man to get a job in the city. Thanks to General Otis, Los Angeles was an employers' paradise. Hours could be as long and pay as low as the employers wished, and no worker could effectively protest.

In 1910 labor decided to make an all-out attempt to unionize Los Angeles. Union organizers came in from other cities. Strikes and riots broke out, and rumors of planned violence began to circulate. Then, in October, the Los Angeles *Times* building was blown up by dynamite.

It happened just after one o'clock in the morning, when the paper was being "put to bed." The force and shock were so great, many thought it was an earthquake, like the one which had devastated San Francisco four years earlier. About a hundred people were still at work. Twenty were

killed outright; scores of others were injured when they
tried to jump out of the burning building. It was discovered later that first there had been a small blast, not in the
building itself but in "Ink Alley," a covered lane in
which the barrels of printing ink were stored. The first blast
ignited some gas leaking from defective pipes, setting off
the major explosion and the fire.

General Otis immediately blamed the unions in a wild
editorial addressed to "you anarchic scum . . . you
leeches upon honest labor . . ." The unions retaliated by
accusing Otis of dynamiting his own building in an attempt
to discredit the unions and collect insurance at the same
time.

For the next few months Los Angeles was like a city
living through a war. It had just suffered one surprise bom-
bardment. When and from what quarter would the next
one come? Wild rumors spread that more atrocities were
planned. Picketing was banned, but workers continued to
go out on strike. General Otis, his military blood almost
visibly boiling over, could be seen riding madly about in
his cannon-equipped car.

The city hired William J. Burns to investigate the explosion. Burns was the head of a detective agency that, like
the Pinkertons, was often hired by employers' groups to
deal with labor problems. By April, 1911, Burns had collected enough evidence to charge three men with the crime:
John J. McNamara, secretary-treasurer of the Structural
Iron Workers Union, his brother James B. McNamara, and
Ortie McManigal, both members of the union. John J. was
arrested in his office in Indianapolis; the other two were

arrested in Detroit. Because of legal difficulties in extraditing them, all three were kidnapped and taken illegally to California, just as Haywood, Moyer, and Pettibone had been illegally transported from Colorado to Idaho.

There were so many similarities between this case and the Idaho case that, when the arrests were made public, the cry went up that this was another attempt to destroy a union, another conspiracy to discredit unionism. And then, as Orchard had done after the Steunenberg killing, McManigal confessed that he and James B. McNamara had dynamited the *Times* building under orders from John J.

Again the country took sides, not only for or against the McNamaras, but for or against organized labor. Newspapers broadcast their views in belligerent editorials and aggressive headlines. Labor leaders and sympathizers were deeply concerned not simply over the fate of the McNamaras, who became labor's newest martyr-heroes, but over the future of unionism.

Samuel Gompers, the founder and president of the American Federation of Labor, was convinced that the McNamaras were innocent and the explosion a deliberate piece of sabotage to stir up antiunion sentiment. The best lawyer in the country must be retained to defend these latest victims of the war against labor.

The best lawyer for the purpose was Clarence Darrow, and to Darrow in Chicago went Samuel Gompers. Darrow, however, though profoundly aware of all the implications of the case and the necessity for a powerful defense, did not want to undertake it himself. He knew it would be an exceptionally difficult contest with powerful antagonists, and he felt he had done his share of fighting. He was no longer young; he had been seriously ill; he was "weary of battling against public opinion." The antiunion and hence anti-Darrow atmosphere in Los Angeles would be far worse than it had been in Boise. He believed a younger, more vigorous man was needed. He knew, also, that the trials would take months, perhaps more than a year, and that his law practice would suffer during his absence.

Other labor leaders and workers throughout the country added their pleas to Gompers'. It became clear that they not only expected Darrow to continue as labor's defender but that his refusal would cast doubt upon the innocence of the McNamaras. It was unthinkable that Darrow should turn his back on labor at such a crucial moment. In the end he had to say Yes because "it would have been harder to say No."

His law partners strongly disapproved of his decision. They felt it was unwise for Darrow to undertake such a difficult case in hostile territory, in a state with whose law he was unfamiliar. Edgar Lee Masters refused to run the office again during another of his partner's prolonged absences. So the firm of Darrow, Masters and Wilson was dissolved. Darrow set up a nominal partnership with one of the younger associates, just to keep his name on the legal register in Chicago. Then he and Ruby closed their apartment and, "with heavy hearts," wrote Darrow, took the train for Los Angeles.

They were greeted in California by a crowd of reporters and other people who for one reason or another wanted to

see the famous Clarence Darrow. From then on till the end
of the case he rarely had a moment to himself.

He assembled a staff of attorneys, rented and furnished
an entire floor in a large office building, and hired a large
corps of investigators. Ruby found a pleasant apartment
for them to live in, but there was little time in which to
relax at home.

One of his associate attorneys was Job Harriman, who
had been temporarily in charge of the case before Darrow's
arrival. Harriman had just been nominated for mayor by
the Socialist-Labor party of Los Angeles. As sympathy for
the McNamaras increased, Harriman's political following
grew, and the fate of the brothers became closely associated with the election.

Toward the end of the summer Gompers arrived in Los
Angeles and went to see the McNamaras in jail. Darrow
had found the brothers, aged twenty-seven and twenty-
eight, pleasant, intelligent, and attractive. One was a devout Catholic, a member of the Knights of Columbus.
Their gentle manner, combined with a candid straightfor-
wardness, seemed to underline their innocence. A final
proof, according to Gompers, was that at the end of his
visit John J. took his hand and said, "I want to assure you
that we are innocent of the crime with which we are
charged."

Gompers spread this message throughout the labor world
and asked for contributions to the defense fund. Thousands of dollars poured in, much of it in quarters and single
dollar bills.

Darrow used a large part of this money to send investigators all over the United States to gather evidence about earlier dynamitings that had occurred in connection with labor troubles. In his confession Ortie McManigal had implicated the McNamaras in many of these. If Darrow could prove some of McManigal's statements false, as he had been able to do with Orchard's confession, it would undermine the prosecution's case.

Another group of investigators went to work gathering information about the long list of prospective jurors. Darrow believed that nothing was more important than picking the right jury. A case could be won or lost on this alone. He always found out as much as he could about the background of the men called for jury duty to make sure of picking those to whose sympathies he could appeal.

Darrow also had inquiries made into the gas leakage which had been going on in the *Times* building for some time before the explosion. He had a small-scale model of the plant constructed and went over it with engineering experts, to determine whether gas, not dynamite, might have caused the explosion. This would mean that the disaster had been caused by careless building supervision or accident, rather than by deliberate sabotage. To prove his point, he planned to explode his little model at the trial.

Like Darrow, the prosecution had also assembled a small army of investigators. Soon Darrow discovered that some of the men whom he had hired were spies for the prosecution. A man on his personal staff turned out to be a Burns detective, who gave the prosecution copies of every report that came into Darrow's office. Then some of the prosecution's agents came to Darrow and offered to sell him copies of information collected by the district attorney. Darrow's telephones were tapped, and detectives shadowed the defense lawyers and witnesses. Throughout the case spying and counterspying went on to such an extent that both sides knew exactly what was going on in each other's offices; each side knew what evidence the other had found; each side, according to one commentator, knew what the other had for breakfast.

As reports came in, Darrow studied them carefully, looking for errors and discrepancies that would discredit Ortie McManigal's confession. But there were no discrepancies. The deeper he dug into the case, the less certain he became of his clients' innocence. And when he learned that the prosecution had unearthed evidence linking the McNamaras with stores of dynamite, his doubts grew.

Was it possible that the McNamaras were not, after all, innocent? The answer, when it came, almost shattered Darrow. He learned that they had indeed dynamited the *Times* building. They had done it, they said, to force public attention to the wrongs committed against labor. But they had not expected such a disastrous result. A very small amount of dynamite had been used, not even enough to damage a printing press directly under the spot where the charge was laid. Only the unlucky coincidence of the gas leak produced the major explosion that had caused the deaths. "It was my intention," said James B. McNamara, "to injure the building and scare the owners. I did not intend to take the life of anyone."

Darrow was faced with a terrible dilemma. What was he to do? By this time, in spite of his efforts to secure a delay, the trial had already begun. The jury was being picked. With the McNamaras guilty, his entire line of defense had crumbled away. He could see that on the strength of the evidence the brothers would almost certainly be found guilty. And they would just as certainly be sentenced to death.

The idea that anyone he was defending might be executed was horrifying to Darrow. He hated capital punishment and carried on a lifelong campaign against it. The state's real motive for putting a criminal to death, he insisted, was not the protection of society but revenge. If the state killed the McNamaras it would not end the struggle between big business and labor; it would only sharpen the antagonism between them and produce more acts of vengeance on both sides.

Should he have the McNamaras plead guilty and hope that in return for a confession the court would impose life imprisonment instead of the death sentence? But suppose the court, pressured by the intense public furor that would surely arise if the McNamaras pleaded guilty, insisted on the death sentence?

It was at this critical moment that the journalist Lincoln Steffens came to Los Angeles. He was among the first and most famous of the muckrakers, the group of journalists who, from around 1902 to 1912, wrote articles exposing corruption in the political and economic life of the country. Steffens had come to Los Angeles to explore the reasons behind the dynamiting. He had been convinced from the start that the McNamaras had done it, as an "act of war" against the employer enemy.

Darrow knew and liked Steffens, and felt that here was someone in whom he could confide. For several days the two men discussed the problem, while Darrow veered between moods of deep depression and cheerful confidence. He would be seized with panic, "scared weak" so that he could hardly walk, reported Steffens. An hour later he would be calm, "humorous, almost gay with self-possession."

In the end Darrow decided that the best solution would be a settlement out of court. A settlement would be the only way of making sure that the McNamaras would not be sentenced to death. Steffens offered to try to arrange one. He believed he could go to the civic leaders and appeal to their spirit of "Christian forgiveness and cooperation" to end the class warfare in Los Angeles. Darrow was skeptical, but agreed to let Steffens try.

After some hard bargaining, the city authorities yielded to Steffens' argument that hanging the McNamaras would not solve anything. The district attorney agreed that if the men pleaded guilty no one would hang. J. B. McNamara, who had done the actual dynamiting, would get life imprisonment; J. J. would get a ten-year sentence. The search for other suspects would be called off, and a conference would be held of capital and labor to deal peaceably with the differences between them.

There was a final conference at the jail to get the McNamaras' agreement to the settlement. Darrow expressed his unhappiness over the penalty they would have to pay as individuals for an act committed for the sake of an organized movement. According to Steffens, the younger brother replied: "But John and I will not be the only ones to suffer. When we plead guilty there will be a shock, and when men are shocked they look for a goat. . . . I've been wondering who will be the real goat, and sometimes I think it will be Darrow."

He was right. Darrow was indeed to be the "goat," and part of the groundwork for this was already being laid. Just as the settlement was being completed, Bert Franklin, one of Darrow's investigators, was arrested on a charge of bribing a juror. He claimed that he had acted under Darrow's orders.

With the McNamara settlement practically arranged, there was no reason to bribe a juror, even if Darrow were capable of such an act. In spite of this, he was accused of conspiring to corrupt a juror. The whole thing looked like a deliberate attempt to discredit him or to give the state a stronger bargaining position.

Lincoln Steffens suggested that dropping the accusation be made part of the settlement, but Darrow refused. He would not allow his personal interests to be linked with a client's. He said the charge should be dealt with separately, after the McNamara affair was finished. Fredericks, the district attorney, was jubilant. He told Steffens that the chance to "get" Clarence Darrow was all the compensation he wanted for giving up the trials of the McNamaras.

There was another consideration that must have led the city leaders to agree to Steffens' plan. For some time they had been worried about the increasing possibility that Job Harriman, the Socialist-Labor candidate for mayor, would win the election. A similar mayor had already been elected in San Francisco. Harriman's leading opponent was the candidate of the Good Government League of Merchants and Manufacturers, known as "the Goo-Goos." This organization, closely identified with General Otis, was already weakened by rumors of fraud and political scandal. Many voters were turning to Harriman as a protest against the Goo-Goos. Others turned to him out of indignation at what they considered the framing of the supposedly innocent McNamaras.

Huge demonstrations were held: twenty thousand people paraded on Labor Day to show their support of Harriman and their opposition to the frame-up. Thousands of Angelenos wore buttons reading "McNamaras Not Guilty!" and "Vote for Harriman!" Even if the McNamaras were tried and found guilty, many people would think they were innocent martyrs and vote all the more enthusiastically for Harriman.

But if the McNamaras should *admit* their guilt—and admit it before the mayoralty election which was about to take place—then Harriman would certainly lose. Even General Otis could recognize this trading advantage. He might lose the satisfaction of seeing the McNamaras hanged, but he would gain the relief of seeing Harriman defeated.

The trial of James B., the younger brother, had been called first. It began on the afternoon of December 1, 1911. For once, in this affair of spies and counterspies, there had been absolutely no leak, no slightest hint that a settlement had been arranged.

When one of the defense attorneys rose and announced in a quiet, matter-of-fact voice that the defendants wanted to change their plea from not guilty to guilty, there was at first no visible reaction. The silence which had been, said Darrow, "profound and ominous" continued for a moment. Then, as Steffens described it: "That court seemed to fly apart; the people in the room scattered with the news, which flew through the crowded streets." Reporters rushed to telephones; soon there were extras all over the country. Men ran outside and shouted the news to the waiting crowds. Many refused to believe it, and fistfights broke out. People raged, wept, swore.

Meanwhile, Darrow remained sitting in the courtroom, exhausted and shaken. At last someone helped him to his feet, and he walked slowly out of the courthouse. An angry crowd was waiting. Some made threatening gestures, others called out words like "Traitor!" A policeman, afraid of possible trouble, took his arm and tried to lead him safely away. But Darrow said: "No, I shall go down the street with the crowd. I have walked with them to the courthouse when they cheered me, and I shall go back the way I came."

And back he went, through the muttering, hostile crowd which had once acclaimed him as their hero and now denounced him as a betrayer. As he walked slowly home in the darkening night, he saw thousands of "McNamara" and "Vote for Harriman" buttons lying on the streets and in the gutters where they had been angrily thrown.

Four days later, the election was held, and Harriman was badly defeated. On election day, also, the McNamaras were formally sentenced. James B. received life, as promised, but John J. was given fifteen years in jail, instead of the ten agreed upon.

Two other agreements were violated. The search for other suspects was not called off; in fact, a new manhunt began, particularly among the leaders of the Structural Iron Workers Union, and several were later jailed. The promised conference which was to inaugurate an era of peace between capital and labor was never held.

Lincoln Steffens was keenly disappointed. His dream of applying the golden rule to labor-employer relationships had failed. Both sides denounced what they considered his interference and folly. Editors refused to buy his work and a labor leader derisively referred to him as "that Golden Rule fellow."

But the real "goat," as J. B. McNamara had predicted, was Darrow. Millions of people all over the country had been convinced of the McNamaras' innocence. Workers had contributed hard-earned money to the defense. They had become so worked up that, when they were suddenly and joltingly proven wrong, they simply could not accept the facts. It was the most devastating shock American labor and its friends ever received, and they were completely unprepared for it. They looked for someone to blame and found Darrow.

He was criticized for not having gone through with the trial. Thousands continued to believe that the McNamaras were innocent and that Darrow had persuaded them to plead guilty for some ignoble reason or other, perhaps money or the hope of getting the jury-bribing charge dropped. The accusation of jury-bribing was made only two days before the McNamaras pleaded guilty. No one knew that negotiations for the plea had been going on for several weeks. It looked as though the plea was a direct result of the bribery charge.

Some people felt that even if the McNamaras were guilty, Darrow should still have had them brought to trial and defended them against the charge. If they had been executed, they would have become martyrs in whose innocence many could have continued to believe, and organized labor would have been saved from the scandal of having a leader openly admit the use of dynamite.

When Gompers heard of the McNamaras' admission, he wept. "I believed the McNamara brothers when they told me they were innocent." Gompers was convinced that labor would lose everything and gain nothing by acts of violence. He felt the McNamaras had set the cause of labor back and wanted nothing more to do with them.

Darrow agreed with Gompers that the McNamaras' act had been a colossal and disastrous blunder, but he would not repudiate them or use them as pawns to serve the needs of the labor movement or of himself.

He believed that a lawyer was like a doctor. His first duty was to save the life of his client. All other considerations must be sacrificed to this.

He knew that if he had brought the men to trial, even if they had been hanged as a result, the workers would have continued to trust him. "I could have done this and saved myself." But he had chosen to save the McNamaras' lives, even though he knew that the very people who had hailed him as labor's defender would turn upon him and accuse him of betrayal.

It was one thing, however, to face the enmity of former admirers; it was another to face the attack of a powerful state. Just as the workers, in their shock and chagrin, blamed Darrow, so the state authorities were at last getting back at the great defender of labor who had so often outwitted them. Both sides were making him the "goat."

In January, 1912, Clarence Darrow was indicted by a grand jury in Los Angeles on two counts of attempted jury bribing. The defender was now the defendant.

17

The Trial of Clarence Darrow

The months of work on the McNamara case had been a depressing experience, but it was nothing to the year of utter torment that now began for Darrow. "Am I dreaming?" he cried at his trial. "And will I awaken and find it all a horrible nightmare, and that no such thing has happened?"

There were the unbelievable charges of jury bribing which could send him to San Quentin penitentiary for ten years and ruin his career. There was the intense strain on his already weakened health and spirit. And there was the rapid depletion of his money with no possible way, under the circumstances, of earning more. Before his ordeal was over, he was more than twenty thousand dollars in debt.

The affair was immensely tangled and filled with inconsistencies and absurdities. Bert Franklin had been hired by

Darrow and put in charge of investigating the backgrounds of prospective jurors because of his long experience in such matters. He had once worked for the city, and it was later said that he was still secretly working for the city, acting as a spy while employed by Darrow.

Two days before the guilty plea was made for the Mc-Namaras, Franklin had been caught giving four thousand dollars to a prospective juror. The money was passed openly on one of the busiest streets in Los Angeles, under the eyes of a couple of city detectives whom Franklin not only knew but actually greeted as he walked toward the corner where "the bribe" was paid. Darrow, in the meantime, had received an urgent telephone call asking him to come to the same corner, just a half block from his office. Later, witnesses would be able to swear that he had been present when the money was paid. In his "confession," Franklin said that another juror had been paid five hundred dollars and attempts had been made to bribe five others. These were to be considered in a separate trial.

The bribes were presumably paid in return for promises to vote not guilty at the McNamara trial. But it had already been settled that there was to be no trial and therefore no jury. Despite the absence of a motive, however, the grand jury indicted Darrow, saying that Franklin had acted on his orders. He was released on twenty thousand dollars bail, an amount that he did not have. Two California friends put up the money for him.

Darrow was stunned by the indictments. He had never really believed the state would go through with the charges. He was already worn out by the difficulties of the McNamara case and longed to go back to Chicago. Now he would have to stay and fight. Where would he find the strength or the money? How would he support himself while his case was being prepared and tried? As a lawyer, he knew it was not enough to be innocent. Proving one's innocence was a long, hard, expensive process, and a highly uncertain one. A courtroom, he was to say later, is not a place where truth and innocence inevitably triumph; it is only an arena where contending lawyers fight, "not for justice, but to win." The adversary system followed in our modern trials was no better than the ancient wager of battle where hired fighters settled legal and moral disputes with their swords. The outcome was determined, not by truth or reason, but by sheer physical skill. The only question settled in a courtroom, he concluded, was the relative strength and cunning of the lawyers.

His first concern, therefore, was to find a skillful lawyer to defend him. The most famous lawyer in California was Earl Rogers. Though he had an almost fabulous reputation, Darrow had never seen him in action, so he and Ruby traveled to a small town in central California where Rogers was trying a case. They slipped into the back row of the courtroom and watched his highly polished performance.

No two lawyers differed more, in their personalities, appearance, courtroom manner, and the way they practiced their profession, than Rogers and Darrow. Rogers was a tall, strikingly handsome man who dressed with extreme care and elegance. Darrow dressed carelessly, almost to the point of sloppiness. His suits were always rumpled, his jacket often left unbuttoned or removed altogether in warm weather, exposing his wide, old-fashioned suspenders, his badly knotted tie was always twisted halfway around his neck, his disheveled hair hung down over the deeply grooved lines in his forehead. Rogers, on the other hand, appeared in court wearing a swallow-tailed coat, silk shirt, jeweled cuff links, an expensive cravat fastened with a diamond stickpin, custom-made shoes, and spats. Instead of ordinary eyeglasses, he sported a lorgnette with a gold frame and long gold handle on a black ribbon, which he used like a stage prop, glaring through it at recalcitrant witnesses or shaking it under the nose of the opposing attorney. Newspapermen called him "a howling swell" and "a dandy," yet he was also, as his young assistant Jerry Giesler said, "dynamic, impressive and dominant."

He exuded charm, self-confidence, and buoyant vitality. Where Darrow moved and spoke slowly, Rogers darted around the courtroom like a gadfly, addressing the witness from every possible angle, often facing the audience or the jury with his back turned toward the witness while he asked him questions. He had an extremely astute and agile mind; he was a master of the art of cross-examination. But he also believed in careful preparation and thorough investigation before coming to court. He often won cases by producing at the most dramatically strategic moment, and like a rabbit out of a magician's hat, a surprise fact or witness upon which the whole case turned. His showmanship, his flamboyance, his clever use of technicalities were in great contrast to Darrow's relaxed, low-keyed, soft-voiced manner, his reliance on persuasive eloquence, and his appeals to the jury's sympathy.

And finally, where Darrow had defended the McNamaras, Rogers was one of the investigating lawyers hired by the prosecution. He had uncovered much of the evidence against the McNamaras. Nevertheless, after watching his brilliant courtroom tactics, Darrow asked Rogers to defend him, and Rogers, who deeply admired Darrow, agreed.

After more than three months of preparation the trial opened on May 15, 1912, and lasted for another three months. With every harrowing day that passed, Darrow sank into a thicker morass of despair. He lost weight steadily until his clothes, which never looked well on him anyway, hung in loose folds around his stooped and dejected frame. Besides the major disaster of the trial and possible imprisonment, there was an increasing worry over money. Rogers charged high fees. No expense was spared for the most detailed pre-trial preparation and research. He also needed a great deal of money for the style in which he lived. He maintained a luxurious home staffed by a corps of servants and gardeners, kept three expensive, chauffeured cars, and was fond of extra flourishes, like taking his daughter and several friends across the continent to New York just to attend a single operatic performance by Caruso.

Darrow was living entirely on his quickly evaporating savings. To stretch the money out as long as possible, he and Ruby moved to a small, cramped apartment and rigorously kept all their expenses, including rent, down to a hundred dollars a month. Even so, he was soon forced to borrow.

The only relief in the continuing nightmare was the solicitous attention of friends. Lincoln Steffens remained in California to encourage Darrow and to serve as his chief witness at the trial. Fremont Older, a leading Los Angeles editor who had helped arrange the McNamara settlement, was another important witness and supporting friend. Fay Lewis, a lifetime friend, left his business and came from Illinois to California just to be at Darrow's side during his ordeal. And there was George Bissett, a man whom Darrow had once saved from a murder charge. Bissett had come from Chicago to Los Angeles, stealing rides on freight cars, to help the man he admired most. When Darrow asked what kind of help he had in mind, Bissett replied seriously that he would kill Franklin, the state's only witness against Darrow; if he were caught, he would gladly take the consequences. "I have had many warm demonstrations of friendship," wrote Darrow, "but this was the first time any man had offered to kill someone for me." He thanked Bissett for this astounding offer, talked him gently out of it, and sent him home.

There were other friends and admirers, however, who turned from Darrow, believing that anyone charged with a crime must be guilty to some degree. He was even more grieved by those friends who continued to be sympathetic and devoted, but showed that they thought it quite possible that he had attempted to bribe the jurors. Darrow was profoundly disturbed to think that people who knew him should so misread his character. He realized bitterly that, even if a jury acquitted him, the aura and suspicion of guilt would always remain. He was overwhelmed by a sense of being caught in a trap from which he could never completely escape.

As he fell deeper into apathy, Earl Rogers became increasingly irritated. In the courtroom Darrow sat day after day slumped dejectedly in his chair, emanating hopelessness. Rogers felt that his client was "a portrait of guilt," and he worried about the impression on the jury: "You look like a dewlapped hound caught in the sheep pen," he complained. Darrow retorted: "You want me to be cheerful when my heart is broken." This was just what Rogers did want, and he tried everything to rouse Darrow. After one furious quarrel about the effect such palpable misery was having on the jury, Rogers shouted that if Darrow did not change, "Then, you lugubrious wretch, you are going to jail!"

Some observers, however, including people on Rogers' own staff, felt that Darrow's unconcealed suffering was rousing a sympathetic response from the jury. But Rogers, a man of resilient spirits, could not stand what his daughter called Darrow's "bleeding gloom and wretchedness." Darrow, in turn, was unhappy about Rogers' line of defense. After every court session there were angry quarrels about Darrow's courtroom behavior and Rogers' courtroom tactics. At the staff conferences Darrow would sometimes break into sobs or Rogers would stalk out in cold fury.

The situation was not helped by the antagonism between Ruby and Adela, Rogers' young daughter who accompanied him everywhere. Each woman felt it her special mission to protect a great man, and they sniped at each other constantly out of mutual dislike and distrust. Adela would talk sharply about the slowness with which the financially pressed Darrows were paying Rogers' fees, and Ruby would comment acidly on Rogers' drinking. Ruby did not share Darrow's respect for Rogers. She considered him altogether too theatrical, "just an actor," not really a lawyer.

Earl Rogers had always been a heavy drinker, and as the strain of the case wore upon him, he turned to his familiar solace. There were times when he failed to show up in his office or at court. An associate would have to take over, and on at least one occasion, Darrow cross-examined witnesses while Rogers was in temporary eclipse. This direct action pulled Darrow out of his lethargic depression for the moment, but the erratic, uncertain behavior of his chief counsel made him more despondent than ever.

The supercharged atmosphere filled the courtroom as well. The lawyers for both the defense and prosecution called each other insulting names, hurled inkwells at the opposition, insolently defied the judge, and barely stopped short of physical violence. William Burns, the detective in charge of the bribery investigation, protested against the way Rogers glared at him through the famous gold lorgnette and demanded that the judge protect him. In turn, Rogers goaded Burns into raising the fancy cane he carried, then insisted that the cane concealed a sword and demanded equal protection from the judge. It was the most violent trial ever held in Southern California, and it went on for three long months into the heat of the summer.

For the first two months Ruby accompanied Darrow through every harrowing day at court and sat by his side during the tense, uncomfortable meals and conferences with Rogers and his daughter. By the middle of July it became too much for her; she had a nervous breakdown and, for a time, had to stay away from the courtroom and rest at home.

When Rogers had been asked to defend Darrow, he had insisted on having complete charge of the case. It had been agreed, however, that Darrow was to make the final summation to the jury. Rogers was not happy about this. He did not entirely approve of Darrow's "courtroom eloquence" or emotional appeals. He felt, too, that Darrow was in no condition to address a jury and would only damage his case.

The night before the final plea, he tried to stir Darrow out of his deep and paralyzing discouragement. Rogers argued, cajoled, threatened, baited him. "At first," wrote Rogers' daughter, "it was like trying to get an elephant out of a wallow." But as the night wore on, "Darrow responded, came to life. . . . The excitement began to get him."

His speech the next day was one of his most powerful. More than a thousand people crowded into the courtroom. At least a thousand more filled the corridors outside. The mob had fought with bailiffs for two hours trying to get into the courtroom to watch the amazing spectacle of Clarence Darrow pleading for himself. Women fainted, and men's clothes were ripped in the intense crush. Reserves from the sheriff's office had to be summoned to maintain order.

At last, Darrow slowly pulled himself out of his chair and walked heavily to the jury box. "Gentlemen of the jury," he began, "an experience like this never came to me before, and of course I cannot say how I will get along with it." He went beyond the technical charge of bribery to what he considered the real purpose of the attack upon him. "What am I on trial for? What is it all about? I am not on trial for having sought to bribe a man. I am on trial because I have been a lover of the poor, a friend of the oppressed, because I have stood by labor for all these years."

Now, he said, the enemies of labor were out "to get" him. "Gentlemen, I say this is not a case of bribery at all."

Nevertheless, he went into the charge of bribery in great detail, taking each statement of the prosecution witnesses and showing it to be false, contradictory, or ridiculous. Even if he were capable of jury bribing, he asked, would he have gone about it as stupidly as the state said he did?

"If you twelve men think that I, with thirty-five years of experience, with all kinds of clients and important cases—if you think that I would pick out a place half a block from my office and send a man with money in his hand in broad daylight to go down on the street corner to pass four thousand dollars, and then skip over to another street corner and pass five hundred dollars—two of the most prominent streets in the city of Los Angeles; if you think I did that . . . why, find me guilty. I certainly belong in some state institution."

On the moral question of whether he was capable of such an act, he said: "I am as fitted for jury bribing as a Methodist preacher for tending bar. By all my training, inclination and habit, I am about the last person in all this world who could possibly have undertaken such a thing."

But even if he had been immoral enough to bribe a juror and stupid enough to do it in broad daylight on the busiest street corner of Los Angeles, while surrounded by detectives, the question still remained: Why? Why should he bribe a juror when it had already been settled that there was to be no jury trial for the McNamaras?

Lincoln Steffens had testified that negotiations for a settlement had started more than a week before the alleged bribery; the terms of the settlement had been accepted by everyone involved four days before the so-called bribery. Once it was decided that there would be no trial and no jury, "is it likely that I would take four thousand dollars of money that was sorely needed, and not only waste that money, but take a chance on the destruction of my life and a term of years in the penitentiary, by sending Franklin down to bribe a juror? Gentlemen, if you can believe it, I do not know what your minds are made of."

Finally, in answer to the accusation that he had had the McNamaras plead guilty just to save his own skin, he went into a long discussion of the McNamara case. He explained the social causes behind it and his reasons for deciding to have them plead guilty. He described his sufferings as a result of that decision.

If he had gone on with their trial, they would have been found guilty and hanged, and that would only have produced more hatred, "so deep, so profound, that it would never die away." But for trying to prevent this, he had drawn upon himself the anger of both sides: "Where I got one word of praise, I got a thousand words of blame!"

By the time he came to the end, after a day and a half, all the people in the courtroom, including the judge and jurors, were weeping. The official court reporter, hardened by years of court attendance, wept so hard he could scarcely write Darrow's words in his notebook. Several women among the spectators sobbed so convulsively they had to be removed.

The jury was out only thirty-four minutes and then returned with a verdict of not guilty. They had agreed on the verdict at once, but thought it would look better to take several ballots before returning to the courtroom.

The crowd went wild with jubilation. Jurors embraced Darrow. The judge came down from the bench to shake his hand. For more than two hours Darrow and Ruby were unable to leave the court while thousands of people came in from the street, where the news had spread, to offer their congratulations. When they were finally able to get through the crowd and go with friends to a restaurant where the celebrations continued, telegrams began arriving from well-wishers all over the United States. A group of workers came with a bouquet of flowers for Ruby. There was general relief at the vindication of Clarence Darrow.

The relief was great, but the ordeal was not quite over. There was still the second count, on which trial was held three months after the first. At the beginning of the second trial Earl Rogers left the case, partly because of illness, partly because both men were weary of the tension caused by the temperamental differences between them. Darrow acted as his own lawyer, assisted by Jerry Giesler from Rogers' office.

The jury was unable to agree, and it looked as though a third trial might be called. By this time all of Darrow's money had gone, together with the twenty thousand dollars borrowed from friends. Once again he was disheartened, feeling that his troubles would never end. Just then a telegram arrived from St. Louis, saying that, since Darrow had spent most of his life defending men for nothing and was now broke, the signer would be happy to send Darrow all the money he needed. It was signed Frederick D. Gardner, a name totally unknown to Darrow.

Darrow's eyes filled with tears when he read the telegram. He had just left the courtroom after the second trial, "sad and discouraged," but when he read the wire it suddenly carried him across the "deep gulf between blank despair and the illusion of hope and comfort and confidence." A few days later a letter arrived from the unknown Mr. Gardner containing a check for a thousand dollars and another from his wife for two hundred dollars.

Soon after, the final indictment against Darrow was dismissed. The two nightmare years in Los Angeles were over. He could go home at last.

18

---·◆·---

Recovery

Back in Chicago, Darrow found his practice completely gone. His old clients made no move to return; there were no new ones waiting for him. As he had feared, the suspicions raised by the charges against him lingered, even though he had been acquitted.

At the age of fifty-six, he had to start all over again. To get enough money for immediate expenses, he sold some of the rare and expensive books he had collected over the years. As another source of income, he turned to lecturing. His first venture was a talk on the German philosopher Nietzsche at the Garrick Theater. When he walked out on the platform, the audience of several thousand who had paid to hear him rose and cheered. He was deeply moved by this demonstration of good will. "One who has serious trouble," he wrote later, "always has two surprises: one

over the friends who drop away, and another at the supposed strangers who stand by him in his hour of need."

The lecture was so successful that the managers of the
Chautauqua movement arranged a long speaking tour for
him. He was well paid and well received. An entirely new
career seemed possible.

Among the "supposed strangers" who had stood by him
was the mysterious Frederick D. Gardner of St. Louis. He
invited Clarence and Ruby to spend a weekend with him
soon after their return to Chicago. Gardner, who was later
twice elected governor of Missouri, and his wife became
close friends of the Darrows.

For a time it looked as though Darrow were through
with law. This was not an altogether unhappy prospect.
For years he had longed to retire and devote himself to
lecturing and writing. But when he was invited to join a
law firm, he found himself tempted to accept.

About twenty years earlier he had given a job to a young
Russian immigrant named Peter Sissman. Sissman never
forgot the opportunity and training Darrow had given him.
Now he had a practice of his own, too small and unimportant, he felt, to interest Darrow. But for Clarence Darrow
to abandon the law seemed to Sissman such a waste that he
offered him a partnership. Darrow was touched by the
offer, yet hesitated. There was, after all, the possibility that
clients would avoid him and he would be of little value even
to Sissman's small firm. It was, however, a chance for a
new beginning, and he agreed.

At first the new partner had so little to do that he spent

more time on the lecture platform than in his law office. But little by little, word got around that Clarence Darrow was back in practice and winning cases again. Clients again found their way to Darrow. By the end of the second year the firm showed a profit, and after four years Darrow was able to pay back all the money he had borrowed during his California trials.

Most of his practice now was straight criminal law. He did much less civil and corporation work than before, and he was no longer labor's principal defender. But a good many of his new clients continued to come from among the poor, who could pay little or nothing for his services. He never turned away anyone in trouble, and there were always enough people in trouble, he said, to keep him in business.

He perfected his trial techniques and became more skilled than ever at cross-examining witnesses and handling juries. His friendly, casual, often chatty manner put even hostile witnesses at their ease, making them relax their guard and tell him what he wanted to know.

During his summations, he carefully watched the jury while he spoke. If their attention seemed to flag, he would drop the point under discussion and switch to something else, returning to the earlier point later on. He would return to each point several times during the course of a single address, with the repetition adding to the total impact. And though he was always serious in presenting a case to the jury, he sensed just when a light or humorous note would be more effective than a formal argument.

He could charm juries into liking and trusting him. He

used simple words and colloquial phrases, seeking not to impress the jurors but to make them understand the situation in terms of their own experiences and emotions. Occasionally he would stretch out a trial to give the jury time to build up a sympathetic attitude toward himself and the defendant. He used to say that juries seldom convicted a defendant they liked or acquitted one they did not like, regardless of the evidence. You don't reason with a jury, he observed. You make them want to acquit the defendant, "and they will find the reason."

A skillful lawyer, Darrow often said, must know how to select the right kind of jurors. The most important quality to look for was "human feeling," a quality influenced by a man's religious beliefs and national origins. On this score he preferred Irishmen above all; they were sure to be emotional, kindly, and sympathetic. Englishmen were pretty good, too, with their long tradition of individual rights. An Englishman was not afraid to stand out alone against other jurors; "in fact, he is never sure that he is right unless the great majority is against him." The German was less interested in individual rights unless his own were concerned; still he, too, was not afraid, and "if he is a Catholic, then he loves music and art; he must be emotional and will want to help you." But the Scotch and the Scandinavians were to be avoided on juries. They were likely to be cold, to know right from wrong and seldom find anything right, and be too concerned about sin and punishment. A juror who laughs is especially desirable; a man who laughs will hate to find anyone guilty. And "the man who is down on his luck, who has trouble, who is more or less a failure, is much kinder to the poor and unfortunate than are the rich and selfish."

Darrow's tactics with opposition lawyers were also carefully worked out. He would disarm them by appearing casual and indifferent. Sometimes he pretended to doze during the course of a trial, lulling the other side into carelessness. Then he would open his eyes, lumber slowly to his feet, and launch an alert counterattack.

In the courtroom he let loose the whole range of his expressive baritone voice. At times he would speak softly and gently, hardly above a whisper, then suddenly swell to an angry roar. He could use his voice to register pity, humility, sorrow, cold logic, or biting scorn.

His features were equally flexible. He would beam, grimace, or scowl at his listeners. Darrow often regretted becoming a lawyer instead of a professional writer, but many who observed him in the courtroom or on the lecture platform said that what he really should have been was an actor. With his client as hero and the facts of the case as plot, he could put on a performance that held the most hard-hearted juror enthralled.

His social life in the large apartment on the Midway was also back in full swing, with many visitors once more coming to enjoy a stimulating evening with Clarence Darrow. To Ruby's annoyance, some of these were women who were attracted to Darrow. Ruby was possessive, flaring into indignant jealousy if any woman received too much attention from Clarence.

He resented Ruby's suspicions and often felt ensnared

by her watchfulness. There were times when he wanted to get away from her. But he appreciated the high level of companionship she gave him and realized that life with Ruby was far happier than life without her. He knew, too, that her irritating behavior was only an expression of the love into which she had channeled her entire life to the exclusion of virtually every other interest or emotion—and it was a love that he returned.

Ruby was as protective as she was possessive. She constantly fussed about his health, his clothes, his food, his sleep. She chose his food carefully, telling him what he must or must not eat, and selected his clothes. All phone calls to their apartment were answered by Ruby, as well as most of the mail. She directed their social life, deciding whom to see or not to see, and when and how long to see them. She made all their travel arrangements and handled details that Darrow would have forgotten or ignored. She voluntarily turned herself into nurse, valet, secretary, confidential assistant. Above all, she constantly told him how much she admired his talents and adored him as a man.

Darrow often complained about this excessive and smothering care. As time went on, however, he began to depend upon it. In the end he enjoyed it.

19

The Right to Speak

Darrow had always been a pacifist, against war and violence. He considered himself a disciple of Tolstoy, the great Russian novelist, who regarded any kind of force as evil. Like Tolstoy, Darrow believed that social problems could and must be solved only through compassion and love. He had often written and lectured on Tolstoy, saying he was one of the chief influences upon his own thinking. In 1903 Darrow wrote a book, *Resist Not Evil,* inspired by Tolstoy's doctrines of nonresistance and nonviolence.

But when World War I broke out and Germany invaded Belgium in the summer of 1914, Darrow found himself feeling far from nonresistant. "I recovered from my pacifism in the twinkling of an eye," he wrote. He was spending that summer in Estes Park, Colorado, with Paul and his three granddaughters. When news of the war reached him, he began to read every scrap of information he could get hold of. He came to the conclusion that Germany was the aggressor. When he read that the German army was marching through Belgium in violation of their treaty, he had "the same reaction that I would experience if a big dog should attack a little one." He wanted the whole world to rise and drive Germany back behind her own borders.

He still hated war; he still respected the principle of nonresistance. But he felt it could be no more than an abstract ideal, a religious doctrine, possible only if everyone practiced it. As man is constituted, nonresistance is unrealistic and even, at times, undesirable. If someone viciously attacks you, he said, you must defend yourself.

Unlike Darrow, the Middle West was largely pro-German, and for a time he was again opposed to the views of those around him. But after Germany began sinking American ships in an attempt to cut off supplies to the Allies, sentiment began to shift. When President Wilson declared war in April, 1917, most of the country swung to his support, and Darrow found himself—for once—in agreement with the majority.

This was the first war in which he was able to believe. He did not, however, allow his convictions to turn him into a professional superpatriot. He liked America best, he wrote, because he happened to have been born there and he understood the language, but he refused to consider it "God's country." God, he said, should be an internationalist, responsible for all countries equally.

His concern with civil liberties remained as strong as ever. He defended the rights of conscientious objectors, feeling that they were entitled to their views though he did not agree with them. And when the war ended in November, 1918, he became involved in some of the crucial civil-rights cases of the period.

In November, 1917, the Bolsheviks seized control of Russia and announced that this was only the beginning of a communist world revolution. By 1919, when German communists held Berlin for several days and Hungarian communists took over Hungary for five months, it looked as though the revolution might very well be spreading beyond the borders of Russia itself. It might even, some Americans feared, cross the Atlantic to the United States.

This fear was intensified by the violent postwar strikes that erupted in 1919, especially among the steel workers, coal miners, and, most surprisingly, the Boston policemen who walked off their posts in protest against intolerably low wages. Fear of revolution reached the point of hysteria when bombs began arriving through the mail to public officials and a series of explosions destroyed homes and buildings. The worst of these occurred in Wall Street in September, 1920, killing thirty-eight people.

Attorney General A. Mitchell Palmer, whose own home had been wrecked by a bomb, went into action against "the Reds." This term included not only communists but socialists and anarchists, despite the fact that these two groups were strongly anticommunist themselves. It included radicals of any description and even outspoken liberals. It became a convenient catchall for unwelcome or unfamiliar persons: labor leaders, foreigners, indeed anyone whose ways or ideas were uncomfortably different.

To carry out his anti-Red campaign, Palmer used a group of laws passed during and immediately after the war. The Espionage and Sedition Acts made it illegal to write, print, or even say anything that might be considered disloyal to the flag, armed forces, government, or Constitution of the United States. Other laws authorized the deportation of aliens. All these laws put severe restrictions on the freedom of speech and press.

Many leading judges and lawyers, including Supreme Court Justices Holmes and Brandeis, objected to the laws, claiming they were unconstitutional and undemocratic. Most of the Supreme Court, however, like the country at large, were caught up in the climate of the period.

On January 2, 1920, Palmer carried out a series of simultaneous raids all over the country, seizing people against whom his agents had any suspicions, however flimsy. Suspects were rounded up in their homes, in labor headquarters, at meetings of organizations considered un-American. Visitors to those already in jail were also arrested. About four thousand were taken into custody. Most of the prisoners were later released, since there was no real evidence against them. More than five hundred were deported after inadequate hearings; others were held for trial.

Clarence Darrow, troubled by the raids, hastened to defend their victims. His own opinion of the accused men and their ideas did not matter; if the rights of one man, whoever he was or whatever he stood for, were violated, the rights of all were endangered. The same unjust law that might serve to trap a guilty person could just as easily be used to silence an innocent one.

His most important espionage case was the defense of twenty members of the newly formed Communist Labor party in Chicago. They had been arrested in the Palmer raids and turned over to the state of Illinois for trial. The prosecuting attorney expressed surprise that Darrow, who had believed in the war, should defend men whose views were so directly opposed to his own. Darrow replied that he had long ago determined never to refuse a case because it was unpopular. He believed that every accused man is entitled to legal help.

His chief purpose in taking the case, however, was to defend freedom, in which he believed above all else. He wanted to turn the trial into a platform for the defense of civil rights. "I shall not argue," he said to the jury, "whether the defendants' ideas are right or wrong. I am not bound to believe them right in order to take their case, and you are not bound to believe them right in order to find them not guilty. . . . I do know this—I know that the humblest and the meanest man who lives, the idlest and the silliest man who lives, should have his say. . . . I am not here to defend their opinions. I am here to defend their right to express their opinions." And again, "If they are wrong, the American people under free discussion can find the wrong."

This time he failed to convince the jury. They found the defendants guilty. Fines and long prison terms were imposed. When the case was appealed to the State Supreme

Court, the verdict and sentences were upheld. Only Chief Justice Orrin Carter dissented, saying that free and open discussion was vitally important in a democracy. Is it better, he asked, to force dissenters "to conspire in silence and secretly?" Would it not be best to allow free discussion about the form of our government and its laws?

Despite the verdicts of the courts, Darrow achieved a victory after all. Before the men began serving their sentences, the governor of Illinois pardoned them, quoting from Justice Carter's opinion in his statement. And in the end, the laws under which they had been convicted were repealed.

During the war, not only radicals but conscientious objectors had been the targets of the Espionage and Sedition Acts. Thousands of Americans were arrested because it was against their religious or moral beliefs to engage in violence. Among them was Darrow's old friend Eugene Debs, who in the previous election had polled nearly a million votes as a Presidential candidate. His sympathies, he told Darrow, were with the Allies, but he was firmly opposed to war, no matter what its cause. He said so openly during a speech, was arrested, and sentenced to ten years imprisonment. Darrow offered to defend him, but Debs refused, saying he could not accept help from anyone who was for the war.

He refused, also, when the war ended, to ask for a pardon. He had done what he thought was right and wanted no concessions from President Wilson. But many others, including Darrow, tried to get him released. Darrow went to Washington to see Attorney General Palmer and then to the federal prison in Atlanta to get Debs's permission to represent him in the pardon proceedings.

Debs greeted him warmly and agreed to let Darrow help him, though he himself would continue to ask nothing from the Administration. Debs and the prison warden were on the best of terms; the warden turned over his own room for the interview. Darrow invited the warden to stay, and the three men spent a pleasant morning, discussing social and political questions. By the time Darrow stirred himself to leave, there was no train back to Washington until late that night. The warden invited him to lunch and the rest of the day was spent in Debs's cell, "the most interesting place in Atlanta." Debs, his five cellmates, Darrow, and the warden sat on boxes, bunks, and chairs, and talked like intimate friends. Darrow was struck by the love of the other prisoners for Debs. There was, he wrote, "the atmosphere of a happy family."

After dinner with the warden, Darrow returned to Washington, confident that Debs would be released at once. But Wilson and Palmer refused. Debs had to wait until the next Administration for President Harding and Attorney General Daugherty to set him free. He was released on Christmas Day, 1921, after nearly three years in jail.

Darrow had always admired and respected Wilson. He felt nothing but distrust for the ineffectual Harding and even less than that for the notorious Daugherty, who was later discharged from office for flagrant misconduct. Yet he always remembered them warmly for releasing Debs while the idealistic Wilson had refused. The whole episode confirmed his belief that no man is all good or all bad, that sometimes better actions come from "bad" than "good" men.

20

---•◆•---

The Loeb-Leopold Case

The idea that all men are mixtures of good and bad appeared in Darrow's next book, *Crime: Its Cause and Treatment*, published in 1922. His purpose in writing it was to give the public a better understanding of crime and criminals, so that a more intelligent, humane, and constructive attitude might be taken toward them. But the book was also an example of Darrow's insistence on looking beneath men's surface behavior to its underlying causes.

He wanted his readers to understand that the criminal was often the victim rather than the enemy of society and should be pitied rather than despised, helped rather than punished. No man, he insisted, is deliberately or innately wicked. He is the result of three factors: heredity, environment, and chance. Since he has no control over these, he should not be held responsible for their results.

Darrow did not believe in free will. He believed that a man was born with a definite physical and mental structure, which might be strong or weak through no fault of his own, and put into an environment, good or bad, which he did not choose for himself. Nor could he choose the accidents of life which brought him the right or wrong companions, the right opportunities or the wrong temptations, the good fortune or the disasters. From beginning to end, man gropes blindly through "the mists and clouds" of chance and accident.

The criminal, said Darrow, is not totally evil. Like all men, he is a mixture of strength and weakness. He resorts to crime when placed under more pressure than he can withstand. The greatest single pressure is poverty, which was why, Darrow found, most lawbreakers came from the poor.

Darrow wanted a new approach to the treatment of criminals. The old system was based on vengeance and punishment. Even after the idea of reform was introduced, punishment was retained on the ground that it would "cure" the criminal or prevent others from committing the same crime.

Prison does not reform a man, said Darrow, it brutalizes or weakens him, leaving him less fit than ever to take his place in society. The only excuse for confinement is the protection of society. But our present system of fixed jail sentences for specific crimes is useless. A criminal should be kept away from society until he is able to adapt himself to it. The exact time will depend not on the crime itself, but on its particular cause and on the treatment of the individual prisoner. To sentence a man to a fixed term like sixty days or ten years is like sending a sick person to a hospital for a time set in advance and then discharging him at the end of that period whether he is cured or not.

Darrow proposed that fixed sentences be done away with. Ideally, a prisoner should be released when it was considered wise and safe to do so. This could be done only if prisoners were put in the hands of experts: physicians, trained criminologists, and above all, he insisted, "the humane."

Every man convicted of a crime should be studied and treated as though he were a sick man in a hospital. He should not be subjected to indignities—prisons should be places, not of degradation, but of rehabilitation. Hope should be held out to him; "his imagination should be enlarged." He should be given vocational training and, when he is ready to leave prison, helped to find a job and to establish himself in a better environment than the one which led him to crime in the first place. While in jail, he should be given work which will pay enough to support himself and his dependents and even, where possible, to compensate the victims of his crime.

Darrow's program called for "intelligence, kindliness, tolerance, sympathy and understanding" on the part of legal authorities and the public. The important thing was to change public opinion about criminals, to make the public accept its responsibility toward them. We should learn to think not of "crime" but of "behavior," to realize that every action has a cause, and that no man must be blamed or punished for the action without considering the cause.

This point of view was to be Darrow's contribution to the American trial system. Lawyers, judges, and juries would no longer be inclined to deal just with *what* was done but would try to understand *why* it was done. Social and psychological circumstances would be considered in arriving at a verdict or sentence. To be sure, this had been done in the past by humane and intelligent authorities, just as it would be neglected in the future by irresponsible ones. The trend to court and prison reform had already been started by men like John Altgeld. But it was Darrow, using the courtroom as a classroom in human understanding and social responsibility, who gave the movement its strongest impetus and its greatest example.

In 1924, Darrow was provided with the most dramatic classroom he had ever had. In the spring of that year two youths, Richard Loeb, eighteen, and Nathan Leopold, Jr., nineteen, kidnapped and killed a fourteen-year-old boy without any apparent motive. They came from respected Chicago families; their fathers were millionaires who gave them unlimited sums of money. Here was one case in which poverty had no part. The crime was utterly senseless, as well as callous and brutal. The public clamored for maximum punishment; they wanted the killers executed without delay.

The Loeb and Leopold families went to Clarence Darrow and begged him to save their sons from the death penalty. Darrow wanted to stay out of the case. He knew that the "shocking and bizarre" crime had set press and public firmly against the defendants. Taking the case would again mean going against public feeling. Darrow, sixty-seven years old "and very weary," had "grown tired of standing in the lean and lonely front line facing the greatest enemy that ever confronted man—public opinion."

But it would be another chance to educate the public, to continue his long campaign against capital punishment. Reluctantly, he accepted so that he might "do what I could for sanity and humanity against the wave of hatred and malice that, as ever, was masquerading under its usual nom de plume: 'Justice.' "

The two accused youths were brilliant students. Leopold was the youngest graduate of the University of Chicago, Loeb the youngest to graduate from the University of Michigan. Leopold was to enter the Harvard Law School in the fall. He had studied fourteen languages, ancient and modern, and was an expert on birds, writing articles and addressing ornithological groups. He had read voraciously in philosophy and literature. Of all the philosophers, Nietzsche, with his concept of the superman, took the greatest hold on his imagination, and he began to think of himself as superior to ordinary men and not bound by the rules and ethics that controlled the actions of lesser beings. This belief was perhaps reinforced by his family's great wealth.

But along with these intimations of superiority, young Leopold also suffered from a sense of inferiority. He may have been an intellectual giant, but physically he was small, weak, and sickly; emotionally, he was far below normal for his age. He was shy and hypersensitive and found it hard to make friends. He adored his mother and was deeply shaken by her death, when he was sixteen. A few years earlier, when his mother was already ill, he had unwisely been put in the care of an emotionally unstable governess who had a disastrous effect upon his development.

His friendship with Loeb began when he was fourteen. Loeb had all the qualities that Leopold admired and felt lacking in himself: good looks, charm, an easy manner. He was tall and athletic. He was very popular and attracted people readily. But beneath his friendly manner, he was cold and hard, caring nothing for others.

Though his parents were immensely wealthy, Loeb had been a neglected and unhappy child. As with Leopold, his parents had provided him with an overabundance of money, but with little guidance of any kind.

He developed an exaggerated fantasy life. At an early age he began to daydream about crime, imagining himself a thief, a master plotter, a leader of an organized gang. Soon he went beyond fantasy and pretense: he actually robbed his friends and went shoplifting for the fun of it. As time went on, he cheated at cards, stole cars, smashed shopwindows, and started several fires. At college he robbed his fraternity house.

He was never caught or even suspected and became convinced that he was clever enough to get away with anything. He grew obsessed with the idea of committing a perfect crime, one which would be difficult, dangerous, and extreme. After intensive thought, he decided upon kidnapping and murder, and asked Leopold to help him. Leopold had helped in several of the earlier thefts and acts of destruction. He did not share Loeb's enjoyment and excitement in committing them; in fact, he disliked the whole business and was always afraid of getting caught. But he admired Loeb and craved his friendship so extravagantly that he was willing to do anything to keep it.

They went on to commit murder. But the "perfect crime" turned out to be a fiasco. The police soon broke the case and arrested them. The deed now assumed its real shape as a monstrous act from whose consequences there was no escape.

Public outrage over the crime was so great that Darrow felt it would be impossible to get an impartial jury. Besides, his only purpose was to get life imprisonment, instead of a death sentence, for the defendants. He had no intention of trying to prove them not guilty, even on the ground of insanity. He decided to waive a jury trial altogether, have them plead guilty, and offer evidence in mitigation of the punishment, as provided by Illinois law. This was done before a judge alone.

The trial opened in July, 1924. Darrow presented the testimony of the medical and psychiatric specialists whom he had summoned to examine his clients in the weeks before the trial. These experts had made a detailed investigation, giving the boys batteries of physical and psychological tests, spending hours questioning them about every aspect of their lives, scrutinizing their every thought, memory, experience. Both were found to have glandular abnormalities and severe emotional disorders dating back to early childhood. The state, trying to prove deliberate and rational premeditation, produced its own psychiatric experts. The legal and psychiatric arguments went on for a month in the broiling summer heat of Chicago, while the world followed every detail as it appeared in lurid newspaper accounts. The case was the greatest sensation of the period, and no one wanted to miss a word. Never before had Darrow's ideas reached so many people.

He began his final summation on August 22. During the trial the courtroom, the corridors, and the sidewalks in front of the courthouse had been packed with crowds. When word got around that Darrow, the Old Lion as the newspapers called him, was to make his closing address, there was practically a mob scene. Policemen were pushed aside while people struggled and fought to get into the courtroom. Women fainted. One of the court attendants had his arm broken. The judge himself could scarcely make his way to the bench. When he finally reached it, he ordered the doors closed. The crowd that remained outside filled every possible inch of the corridors and stairways of the building, while hundreds more gathered in the surrounding streets.

Darrow's address took twelve hours, spread over three days. Throughout, he kept returning to the dangerous pressure of public opinion. If it were not for that, he stressed, a life sentence would have been routine. In the history of Illinois, no one under the age of twenty-three had ever been given the death sentence after a plea of guilty. If the boys had been poor, there would have been no argument necessary; they would have been sentenced to life imprisonment as a matter of course.

But the public, antagonized by the boys' wealth, insisted that they must not be allowed to "buy their lives." If the judge yielded to the public clamor and, violating all legal precedent, sentenced the boys to death, it would be only because of their money: "If your honor shall doom them to die, it will be because they are the sons of the rich." They would die, not for lack of money, but on account of it, which would be equally unjust.

He pleaded with the judge to exercise his independent judgment, his understanding, and his courage, and to decide upon the sentence without any concern for the demands or threats of a vengeful public.

Darrow made no attempt to gloss over the atrocity of the crime. He openly acknowledged and even described in detail every incident of the terrible affair. He did not expect or want his clients to escape the consequences of their act. "Neither the parents nor the attorneys would want these boys released. . . . Those closest to them know perfectly well that they should not be released, and that they should be permanently isolated from society."

What he wanted was to make the judge—and the public—understand that the defendants were not fully responsible for their acts and should therefore not receive maximum punishment. He wanted to diminish the intense force of the public's hatred which, at its height, would be satisfied with nothing less than the death of Loeb and Leopold.

He challenged the state's claim that it was a deliberately planned, cold-blooded murder, "the sane act of sane men." It was, said Darrow, the senseless, terrible act "of immature and diseased brains," which were the result of conditions of heredity and environment over which they had no control. This theory of cause and effect beyond the individual's control had been a central theme of his book on crime.

What, after all, was he asking that made the public so indignant? Only that two boys, eighteen and nineteen, "be permitted to live in silence and solitude and disgrace and spend all their days in the penitentiary."

Capital punishment, he argued in an impassioned conclusion, was useless and inhumane. Punishment does not deter crime. Crime is an illness whose only cure is to find and remove the cause. Execution is nothing but a barbaric act of revenge, a form of public bloodletting.

Killing is evil, said Darrow, no matter who does it. It is bad enough when done as the mad act of a pair of abnormal boys; it is monstrous when done deliberately by the state. The state must be more civilized, more intelligent, more humane than unbalanced killers.

Do you think, asked Darrow, that you can cure the hatreds and maladjustments of the world by killing those whose warped lives have led them to crime? Would it not be better to use understanding and love? "I am pleading," he said, "that we overcome cruelty with kindness, and hatred with love."

When Darrow finished, there was absolute silence in the hot, airless, overcrowded courtroom. The judge was weeping openly, and there were tears in the eyes of many of the listeners.

Three weeks later the court again convened to hear the judge's decision. Again the crowds fought to get in and massed in the corridors and streets. Darrow and everyone else connected with the defense were brought in under heavy police protection. No one had the slightest inkling of what the decision would be, and again the room fell tensely still as the judge began to speak. He pronounced the sentence of life imprisonment, adding that though the public had demanded the more dramatic penalty of death, "the prolonged suffering of years of confinement may well be the severer form of retribution and expiation."

The crowd rushed out to spread the news. Darrow remained until the courthouse and streets were almost empty. Then he walked slowly to a waiting car and went home.

The case had been a grueling strain. He was exhausted from the long hours of preparation and conferences and from the pressure of public disapproval. He had received hundreds of abusive letters from people who identified the attorney with the criminals. He was severely criticized for taking the case, even by those who should have accepted the principle of providing a defense for every accused person.

He was accused by some people of "selling out," of defending a pair of atrocious killers just for the money, since it was assumed that such wealthy families would pay a fortune for his services. Rumors mentioned fees of up to two million dollars. To prevent such accusations, Darrow announced at the outset that he would let the fee be determined by the Chicago Bar Association.

When the Loeb and Leopold families had first begged Darrow to help them, they had been willing to promise anything. After it was all over, however, they began to dicker and haggle over the fee, refusing to submit it, as agreed, to the Bar Association, saying the association would be prejudiced in Darrow's favor as a fellow lawyer.

At last they sent a check for thirty thousand dollars, a relatively small sum under the circumstances, especially since it was thought that the Bar Association would have awarded a hundred thousand dollars. Darrow knew he could have sued and collected a suitable fee, but he found the negotiations so distasteful that he accepted the check just to bring the matter to an end.

Besides, he had already achieved his real aims in taking the case. He had scored another point against capital punishment; he had pioneered in introducing into the courtroom medical and psychological evidence presented by experts. He had given the law courts and the public another lesson in his theory of cause and effect. He had made them consider not just the crime as such but the human beings who committed it and the conditioning factors that produced it. In pronouncing sentence, the judge had said: "The careful analysis of the life history of the defendants and of their present mental, emotional and ethical condition has been of extreme interest and is a valuable contribution to criminology."

Darrow's handling of the case would profoundly influence the practice of American criminal law.

21

---◆---

Darwin in Tennessee

During each long and difficult case, Clarence Darrow would decide to retire. He would tell himself that this was his last. As time went on, he had less respect for legal procedures. He was bored and irritated with the waste of time, the delays, deceit, quibbles, "the endless palaver" during which "the substance is lost in technicalities." And he was tired. He no longer wanted to "fight in a courthouse all day and study and contrive far into the night."

He greatly preferred public speaking. After the Loeb-Leopold case he found himself deluged with invitations to lecture and debate. He had become more famous than ever. Before the trial there may have been people in the United States who had not heard of Clarence Darrow. After it, there could have been none who did not at least know his name, and everyone was eager to see in person America's most celebrated defender of unpopular causes.

He set off on a speaking tour of the country. His audiences loved his manner of talking directly and frankly to them as though he were engaging each listener in a private conversation. They liked the humor with which he exposed his opponents' ideas and the irony which he frequently directed at himself. He spoke in a slow, deep, Midwestern drawl, which was often compared to Abraham Lincoln's, with the same humorous chuckle and the same misleading impression of easy-going laziness covering a quick, shrewd brain. He always seemed to be enjoying himself on the platform; his audience and even his opponents shared his enjoyment.

Physically, he had changed little over the years. The lines in his face were more sharply cut; the blue eyes may have seemed more deep-set than before, but they shone with as much warmth as ever. The hair on his massive head had become grayer and thinner, but the unruly lock still fell down over the side of his large forehead. He often twisted the lock as he spoke, or shrugged his broad, sloping shoulders to emphasize a point. Sometimes he hitched his thumbs through the top of his old-fashioned suspenders, or put his hands deep into the pockets of his baggy pants. His clothes, and the comments of reporters on them, were Ruby's despair. No matter how expensive or perfectly tailored they were, no matter how often she had them cleaned and pressed, they always looked worn and rumpled, as though he had slept in them. She bought him the best shirts and kept them immaculately laundered, but he somehow managed to make them look like limp rags once they were draped on his large frame.

He might have gone on indefinitely making speeches, but in 1925, scarcely a year after the Loeb-Leopold affair, a surprising thing happened. A case of great public interest arose, and Clarence Darrow volunteered his services. Generally, he had to be urged or drafted into controversial cases. Several times he had declared himself through with fighting public opinion. Here he would be once again opposing massive public sentiment, yet he actually wanted and offered to lead the fight.

The issue this time was not crime or labor but science. One of the most dramatic clashes of the 1920's was over Darwin's theory of evolution, which taught that all life had evolved from simple one-celled creatures into higher and more complex forms including man himself. This was angrily rejected by those who accepted the story of the creation of Adam and Eve exactly as given in the Bible. The fundamentalists, those who believed literally in the Bible, regarded the theory of evolution as dangerously antireligious. They insisted that every word in Scripture must be taken as literally and exactly true. Man had never evolved, they argued. He had always been man, created in the image of God.

For the evolutionists to deny this was bad enough, but the fundamentalists were further incensed because of their mistaken belief that Darwin claimed that men had descended from monkeys. This idea became the catch phrase for the whole controversy.

A fundamentalist anti-evolution movement was organized

to combat the teaching of evolution in American schools. In 1920 William Jennings Bryan, convinced that the theory of evolution was undermining the religious faith and moral fiber of the younger generation, joined and became its leader. From then on, it swept through the country, taking concrete action by getting state legislatures to ban the teaching of evolution in public schools. Indeed, anything not explicitly stated in the Bible was suspect. In 1922 a teacher in Kentucky was fired for teaching that the earth was round. In 1923 Oklahoma passed a law forbidding public schools to use any book containing Darwin's theory. Florida, now Bryan's home state, passed a resolution written by Bryan himself forbidding the teaching of evolution, which it identified with agnosticism and atheism. In Texas and Kentucky, though similar bills failed to pass, several college professors were fired for their views on evolution. In 1924 a biology textbook was banned in North Carolina because the governor did not want his daughter to use a book "that prints pictures of a monkey and a man on the same page."

In 1925 Tennessee passed an anti-evolution law which forbade the teaching of any theory that denied the story of Creation as contained in Genesis and taught instead that man had descended from a lower order of animals. When the Tennessee law was passed, the American Civil Liberties Union announced that it would finance a case to test its constitutionality. Several citizens of Dayton, Tennessee, opposed to the law decided to take advantage of the offer. They persuaded John T. Scopes, a young high school biology teacher, to let himself be arrested for teaching evolution.

William Jennings Bryan immediately offered his services to the prosecution. After his third defeat for the Presidency, his political influence had declined sharply, and his interests shifted from politics to religion. He worried about the growing religious skepticism of the young and felt called upon to provide them with moral guidance. He spent more and more of his time addressing YMCAs, church gatherings, and Chautauqua audiences. His favorite lectures, delivered in the voice which still retained its spellbinding power, were a mixture of politics and religion. In 1915, having served briefly and not very happily as President Wilson's Secretary of State, he had taken up the cause of prohibition, calling it "a veritable religious crusade," and traveled about the country urging his listeners to take action against "the curse of drink."

The adoption of the Prohibition Amendment in 1919 left him again without a cause. He had settled in Florida where he divided his energies mainly between conducting a Sunday School class and helping the Florida real estate boom. His Sunday School class in Miami drew thousands of listeners, too many for an indoor hall; it had to be moved to the Royal Palm Park where often as many as eight thousand people gathered to hear him talk. His lectures for a real estate company drew smaller audiences but paid him well, two hundred and fifty dollars per lecture. Neither of these, however, quite satisfied his sense of mission, and he toyed with a series of moral reforms until at last the anti-evolution crusade came to fill the void. He began traveling around the country urging legislatures to make the teaching of evolution a crime. The Tennessee law was one of his triumphs. Now that it was to be tested in the courts, who could speak up for it more eloquently than Bryan, the arch anti-evolutionist himself?

When Clarence Darrow heard that Bryan was to help the prosecution in the Scopes trial, he offered his own services to the defense without payment. He not only refused a fee; he paid his own expenses, which came to two thousand dollars. He felt that Bryan and the fundamentalists were a threat to education and to free scientific inquiry, and that the country must be roused to the danger.

With Bryan and Darrow facing each other, the case received maximum publicity. Reporters flocked to Dayton from all parts of America and even from abroad to attend this clash of opposing giants, this duel between the unyielding orthodoxy of Bryan and the flexible rationalism of Darrow. Some people saw it as the battle of the century between righteousness and sin; others considered it a contest between the old ways of thinking and the new.

To Bryan himself, it also appeared as a contest between simple country virtue and city sophistication. In 1896 he had made a speech in New York City which turned out to be one of his rare failures as a spellbinder. Many of his bored listeners walked out before he was finished, and the newspaper reports dismissed him as either a cheap or a dull orator. For the rest of his life Bryan hated New York and associated large cities with corrupt cynicism. He welcomed the opportunity to appear as the champion of the pure-hearted and pure-minded countryfolk of Tennessee against the big-city lawyers. In addition to Darrow, the defense included Arthur Garfield Hays and Dudley Field Malone, both prominent New York attorneys active in liberal movements.

To the town of Dayton the whole affair was a grand show, a holiday, almost a circus. The town's boosters saw a chance to attract business and "put the town on the map." They prepared for the trial as for a World's Fair. Lawns and gardens were spruced up. The local hotel and store-keepers painted their building fronts and decorated them with banners. More banners and signs, most of them with religious admonitions like "Sweethearts, Come to Jesus" and "Prepare to Meet Thy Maker," were attached to fences or swung between trees or arched above streets. A drugstore advertised a "Monkey Fizz." Stands selling hot dogs, ice cream, sandwiches, soft drinks, watermelons, and religious books were set up on the streets leading to the courthouse. On the courthouse hung a sign saying "Read Your Bible," while inside the building telephone booths and radio equipment were installed for the use of newspaper reporters. This was to be the first trial ever broadcast over the newly developed commercial radio.

Crowds of people poured in. Tennessee mountaineers came down out of the hills to the "wicked town" of Dayton (population eighteen hundred), to witness the battle against sin. Some of the men carried rifles as they moved sternly and soberly about the town in their horse-drawn wagons. Revival groups set up tents. Reporters and out-of-state spectators were everywhere, to the delight and profit of the townspeople.

When Bryan arrived in Dayton, an exuberant crowd gathered at the station to welcome their hero. They saw an aging, overweight man, with glittering eyes above a thin-lipped, extraordinarily wide mouth. When he smiled, his mouth stretched almost clear across his face, moving one observer to remark: "That man can whisper in his own ear."

Later, when he strolled through the streets of Dayton, he wore a white pith helmet, carried a palm-leaf fan, and usually had his pockets stuffed with radishes, his favorite vegetable, which he constantly munched. Bryan loved to eat and found it hard to stop nibbling between his gargantuan meals.

Darrow arrived two days later, on the night before the trial opened. There was no official welcome for him, but he was greeted with friendliness by the people who had come out of curiosity. Scopes met him at the station, shook hands warmly, and then took him off to the Mansion, an eighteen-room house just outside the town. It had been vacant for several years, had no lighting, no screens, and inadequate plumbing. Scopes and his friends had fixed it up for the defense lawyers and the scientists—anthropologists, zoologists, geologists—who had come to testify at the trial. When Ruby arrived, after the trial began, she immediately made other living arrangements, charming the town banker into turning his house over to the Darrows for their personal use. With the help of friendly neighbors, she wrestled with the problem of getting fresh food and especially ice. Local sources could scarcely meet the heavy demands of the thousands of outsiders in Dayton.

Though comfortably set up in his own house, Darrow continued to spend a good deal of time at the Mansion, sitting on its pleasant open porch or in its sparsely furnished living room to confer with the other defense lawyers and the scientific witnesses, or to chat with reporters and friends who gathered around as though it were a social event.

The whole atmosphere was less that of a serious legal affair than of a public gathering, a convention, or, most of all, a religious revival meeting. Every night popcorn merchants and street-corner magicians raised their voices in competition with the evangelists who exhorted the swarming crowds to repent and be saved. Dayton, commented one reporter, "was drunk on religious excitement." Just outside the town, a group of Holy Rollers drew large audiences by their frenzied shouting, singing, and dancing. Their views of Darrow and his colleagues were expressed by cries of "The Lord hates lawyers" and "I know my young ones are in glory because I never learned them nothing, Glory to our Lord!" On Sundays and sometimes on weekday evenings as well, Bryan delivered sermons in several Dayton churches. One Sunday Darrow himself gave a lecture on Tolstoy before an audience of two thousand in nearby Chattanooga.

The trial opened on July 10, 1925. Presiding over the freshly painted courtroom was Judge John T. Raulston—

tall, broad-shouldered, red-faced, perpetually smiling—
who described himself as "jist a reg'lar mountin'eer Jedge."
Above his head was a large sign, "Read Your Bible Daily."
The judge had entered carrying a Bible in one hand and a
palm-leaf fan in the other. Almost everyone in court waved
fans throughout the proceedings.

The day was extremely hot. Darrow said the crust under
the sin-fearing town must be very thin; where else could
"such hellish heat" come from? The courtroom was made
even hotter by the presence of the crowd which filled every
available seat and lined the walls. Many brought their
lunches, knowing that if they left the courtroom at the
lunch recess, their seats would be grabbed by others waiting outside. Those who could not get in sat on the lawn,
where loudspeakers broadcast the court proceedings.

Practically everyone, including the judge, was in shirtsleeves, increasing the air of informality. When Bryan entered, the entire assemblage applauded and Bryan bowed
and smiled. The judge had come accompanied by members
of his family carrying flowers. After he took his place on
the bench, all the attorneys, both prosecution and defense,
grouped themselves around him and photographs were
taken. While they were posing, Judge Raulston felt that
someone was missing. Of course—the defendant, whom
everyone seemed to have forgotten in the excitement over
Bryan and Darrow. "Come up here, Scopes," called the
judge. Young Scopes, tall, blond, looking especially youth-
ful in a blue shirt with a bow tie, joined the smiling group.
The judge enjoyed having his picture taken and permitted
news photographers to interrupt the proceedings all through

the trial with requests for the participants to move themselves or turn their heads for better camera shots.

The session opened formally with a prayer delivered by a minister who invoked God's blessing on the court, the jury, and the attorneys—even the "foreign" attorneys. In his forty-seven years of trial practice, Darrow had never seen a court opened with a prayer. The judge added a few words of welcome for the "foreigners."

Darrow and the other defense lawyers were given the honorary title of "Colonel"; the prosecution attorneys were called "General." Throughout the trial, the atmosphere seesawed between honeyed exchanges of compliments and acrimonious slinging of insults.

It was clear from the beginning that the anti-evolution law, not Scopes, was on trial. Or as Darrow put it, "Scopes isn't on trial; civilization is on trial."

The state claimed that since the public supported the schools and paid teachers' salaries, it had a right to tell the teachers what to say and do. "The hand that writes the pay check rules the school," Bryan said. The public was under no obligation to pay a teacher who was undermining the religious faith of their children. The theory of evolution was, in the eyes of Tennessee, contrary to the Bible and hence antireligious. This was Bryan's chief emphasis throughout his anti-evolution crusade: to him, people who believed in evolution, indeed all scientists, were agnostics or atheists.

To Bryan, it was science versus religion. "You believe in the age of rocks," he used to say, "I believe in the Rock of Ages."

The defense wanted to show that science and religion were not opposed to each other and that teaching evolution did not undermine religious faith. To show this, they had to explain evolution, and it was for this reason that scientists had been brought to Dayton to testify. The attorneys for Scopes pointed out that millions of people, including preachers as well as scientists, believed in both religion and science. Many of the defense lawyers and scientists were themselves devout believers in God.

Above all, the defense wanted to stress the importance of removing legal restrictions on the freedom to think and to teach. The state might say what subjects should be taught, but it had no right to insist that they be taught falsely. The state must not prevent the geography teacher from saying the earth is round; the state must not rule that two and two make five in mathematics. In the teaching of biology the state must permit the inclusion of evolution, a theory fully accepted by scientists, as the defense planned to demonstrate.

Furthermore, the defense argued, the state was violating the constitutional guarantees of freedom of religion, since it insisted that only the fundamentalist interpretation of a particular version of the Bible be used as a yardstick to measure what should or should not be taught. What about citizens who were Protestants but not fundamentalists, or who were Catholic or Jewish? What about Mohammedans whose holy book was the Koran, not the Bible? Or Buddhists, not to mention those who had the constitutional right to no religion at all? Wasn't the state interfering with their religious freedom?

The law was improperly vague in saying only "the Bible."
What Bible? asked the defense. The King James version
used by Protestants? The Douai version used by Catho-
lics? There were other versions as well. And all of them,
the defense pointed out, were only translations of translations of the original Hebrew, Aramaic, and Greek texts,
which had been lost.

Many of those in the courtroom were thrown into confusion. This was the first they had heard of more than one
Bible. Nor had they ever before thought of what might
happen to the meaning of a book in the process of translation.

During the trial the defense group met at the Mansion
for classes in translation conducted by Rabbi Herman
Rosenwasser, who had been brought to Dayton as a Bible
expert. He would take a passage from a Hebrew copy of
Genesis, translate it into German, giving several possible
words for each Hebrew word, and then translate from German into English, again giving all the English words that
could be used for each German word. The result was a
variety of possible meanings, all derived from the same
Hebrew passage. The statement that God "created" the
earth, for example, could just as properly say, after going
through several translations, that God "evolved" it.

Darrow hammered away at all these points in his opening
speech. The Bible, he went on to say, is not a book of geol-
ogy or biology; it was written long before the discoveries
of modern science. It is primarily a book of religion and
morals; it was never intended as a scientific textbook.

The constitution of Tennessee gave men the right to differ about religion when it said that no act shall be passed to interfere with religious liberty and that all men had the right to worship according to their own conscience. To demand that biology be taught only according to the fundamentalist conscience was to deny religious liberty to all nonfundamentalists and was therefore unconstitutional.

He concluded with a plea for tolerance, intellectual freedom, and the right to be different. "To think is to differ," he said. If you discourage difference, you discourage thought. If today you make it a crime to teach evolution, tomorrow you may ban books and newspapers. After that we will be "marching backward to the glorious ages of the sixteenth century when bigots lighted fagots to burn the men who dared bring any intelligence and enlightenment and culture to the human mind."

When Darrow finished, court was adjourned for the day. As he walked out of the courtroom with Ruby, a woman looked at him and said, "The damned infidel!" But one of the opposition attorneys threw his arms around Darrow, saying, "It was the greatest speech I ever heard in my life on any subject." Other citizens of Dayton came up to congratulate him. He was winning them over by his combination of informality, personal charm, and impressive oratory. A group was formed to pray for him daily.

But there were still many who regarded him with suspicion. During the afternoon the town's water supply had stopped functioning; that evening the electric current failed, and later on there were flashes of lightning and thunder. The next morning many townspeople looked askance at Darrow, as though he were bringing the wrath of God upon them.

They were really stunned, however, when Darrow stood up in court that morning, on the day following his opening speech, and said he objected to the prayer which opened each court session. He asked that it be dropped, arguing that since the case involved religious issues, prayers were neither fair nor suitable, in addition to being without legal precedent. He had no objection to anyone in the courtroom praying privately, but the court itself should not be turned into a meetinghouse. The judge, the prosecuting attorneys, and the spectators were indignant. To object to prayers upon any occasion was unheard of. This was really a direct challenge to Divine Providence, and if the thunder had broken out and the lights and water ceased functioning again, the townspeople would not have been in the least surprised. Judge Raulston overruled Darrow's objection, and every session of the trial continued to be opened with a prayer. Each time it was offered by a different preacher, selected by a committee of church members appointed by the court for that specific purpose.

With that settled, the day's prayer was offered, and then a fifteen-minute recess was called so that news photographers could take pictures.

On the following day the state called its witnesses to the stand. One of the first was a fourteen-year-old high-school student who testified that Scopes had taught evolution in the classroom and had taught also that man was classified as a mammal. When the attorney general asked if Scopes had explained what a mammal was, many of the people in the courtroom were shocked. One woman covered her ears, and several children who had come with their parents were sent out of the room. The youngsters ran downstairs to the lawn where they listened to the loudspeakers which carried every word from the courtroom to the crowd outside.

The next witness was a seventeen-year-old student who, in reply to Darrow's questions, said he had belonged to a church both before and after he had been in Scopes's class. Darrow asked him: "You didn't leave church when he told you all forms of life began with a single cell?" No, not at all, was the reply.

The next day Bryan said he refused to be classified as a mammal. He picked up a copy of the biology textbook used by Scopes and showed the court a diagram of the evolutionary tree. Each class of animals was in a separate circle, with the number of species in that class written in the circle. In the one marked mammals, there were 3,500 species. Since man is a mammal, this meant that he had to share the circle with 3,499 other species. "How dared those scientists," stormed Bryan, "put man in a little ring like that with lions and tigers and everything that is bad!"

This was Bryan's first real speech in the trial and he made the most of it, becoming florid and emotional, declaring that the study of evolution destroyed not only religious faith but all moral standards. There were cheers and amens from his audience.

When Darrow called his first witness for the defense, Dr. Maynard M. Metcalf, an eminent zoologist, the crucial legal argument of the whole trial was set off. The prosecution objected to having scientists explain evolution. They said it had nothing to do with the trial, which was simply a matter of determining whether Scopes had violated the law. Darrow felt that the jury could not determine whether the theory of evolution violated the law unless they knew something about evolution, and his purpose in calling the scientists was to provide this knowledge. He also planned to show that the evidence for evolution was so great that the anti-evolution law was not "a reasonable exercise of the police power."

The lawyers for both sides wrangled over the legal issue involved. Finally Judge Raulston agreed to listen provisionally to the first expert witness without the jury present, in order to determine whether scientific evidence would be admissible.

Dr. Metcalf began by saying, in response to Darrow's questions, that he was both a member of the Congregational Church and a believer in evolution. He was sure that every zoologist, botanist, and geologist in the United States accepted evolution. Then he proceeded to give the most extraordinary information his listeners had ever heard or dreamed of. He traced the geological history of the earth and outlined the story of evolution to an awe-struck and incredulous audience. When he said that life had existed six hundred million years ago, the judge gasped, said one writer, "and took a long drink of water."

When the time came for his ruling, Judge Raulston declared that scientific testimony was not relevant to the case and would not, therefore, be permitted. Darrow was furious.

Such a ruling would cut out the entire defense argument.

The defense was then told they could submit written statements of what they expected the scientific witnesses to prove. Darrow asked that the court be adjourned for the rest of the day so that the defense lawyers would have time to draw up these statements. When the judge began to argue the point, Darrow angrily interrupted, saying that he did not understand why every request of the prosecution should be given an endless amount of time and consideration while every suggestion of the defense, however competent, was immediately overruled.

The judge replied, "I hope you don't think the court is trying to be unfair." Darrow pulled on his suspender strap and slowly drawled out, "Well, Your Honor has the right to hope."

The judge turned red and retorted, "I have the right to do something else, perhaps."

"All right, all right," said Darrow impatiently. He folded his arms and waited, while a silence fell over the room. Most of the reporters thought Darrow would be jailed for contempt of court. But Judge Raulston, too angry perhaps for further action, declared the session adjourned.

The hostile exchange took place on a Friday. Over the weekend there was more excitement and tension than ever, while the incident was discussed all over town. To defy a judge was considered in that area almost as outrageous as to question court prayers. On Monday morning Judge Raulston, still angry, declared that Darrow's behavior had been an insult to the court and to Tennessee, "one of the greatest states in the union." Darrow was cited for contempt and instructed to post a bond for five thousand dollars. A spectator from Chattanooga offered to put up the money.

After the lunch recess Darrow rose and, in the most affable and gentle way, apologized for his behavior on Friday. He explained that the words had slipped out without premeditation, that he loved the people of Tennessee and had received nothing but courteous treatment from them, and that he had not the slightest fault to find with the court. He had not realized, he said, just how his words had sounded until he read the transcript of Friday's proceedings. "The remark should not have been made . . . and I am sorry that I made it." The people in the courtroom cheered.

Judge Raulston then delivered a little sermon, ending with: "My friends and Colonel Darrow, the Man that I believe came into the world to save man from sin . . . taught that it was godly to forgive. I accept Colonel Darrow's apology."

There was applause from the relieved spectators.

Before the trial could continue, the judge announced that the heavy weight of the crowds in the courtroom had caused cracks to appear in the ceiling of the room below. There was some danger that the floor might collapse altogether. It had been decided, therefore, to transfer the court to the lawn. Judge, lawyers, spectators rose and moved outdoors.

Now the trial really took on the aspect of a public entertainment or sports event. The chief performers—the judge and attorneys—sat on a wooden platform that had been built against the courthouse wall. Massed around them sat several thousand people on rough wooden benches or on the bare ground. The front rows were reserved for the jury and the newspapermen. Over to one side, like rooters at a ball game, sat a large group of young people, devoted admirers of Darrow. They were balanced on the other side by a group of stern-faced fundamentalists, supporters of Bryan. Those who had been unable to crowd into the courtyard sat on the roofs of cars parked outside the fence; others leaned out of the courthouse windows, and some of the younger listeners climbed trees and sat on the branches. Boys selling soda-pop and snacks pushed through the crowd. Some of the spectators were sheltered by the spreading maple trees of the courthouse lawn; most of them sweltered under the hot July sun.

When the audience had settled itself comfortably, Arthur Garfield Hays read the statements prepared by the scientists on the meaning and proof of evolution and its relation to religion. Judge Raulston had ruled earlier that the jury would not be permitted to hear this. But Darrow felt that the statements served an important purpose. They educated the public on the meaning of evolution and perhaps on the importance of freedom in education and scientific research. The jury may have been barred from Darrow's classroom, but the American public received every word of the lesson since every word was printed by newspapers throughout the country.

After the scientific statements were read and put into the record, the judge ordered the jury to return. Darrow rose to his feet and entered a protest which again outraged the assemblage. On the wall of the courthouse, directly facing the jurors' benches, was a sign ten feet long. It said "Read Your Bible," and pointing to the word "Bible" was a large hand. Darrow insisted that the sign be removed because it might prejudice the jury. Shock rippled over the crowd; the prosecution attorneys leaped up in fury. One of them called the defense "a force that is aligned with the devil and his satellites." Objections and counterobjections were flung across the platform while the audience joined in the debate and the bailiff rapped for order, calling out, "This is no circus! There are no monkeys up here!"

The judge finally ordered the sign removed. Once more the crowd settled down. Then Arthur Garfield Hays announced that the defense wanted to call another expert witness, an acknowledged authority on the Bible, William Jennings Bryan himself.

Here was the high point of the trial. Everything else had been a prelude to this dramatic climax when Bryan and Darrow confronted each other, the defender of pure faith and the upholder of reason and scientific inquiry.

The judge could have ruled against Bryan's testifying, as he had ruled against the personal appearance of the scientists and theologians for the defense. But Judge Raulston was as eager as anyone else to watch the giants battle face to face. He promised Bryan that Darrow and the other defense lawyers could be called as witnesses also. Bryan then agreed to testify and, carrying his palm-leaf fan, walked to the witness stand.

Darrow sprawled comfortably in a chair, with an open Bible on his knees, and peered benevolently at Bryan over the tops of his gold-rimmed eyeglasses. Both men were in shirtsleeves. In the gentlest of voices, Darrow asked Bryan whether he took every word in the Bible literally. In answer to Darrow's questions Bryan said yes, Jonah was swallowed by a big fish and Joshua did make the sun stand still so that the day would be longer. After an argument over these points, Bryan admitted that, since the sun does not go around the earth, it would have to be the earth, not the sun, that stood still. Darrow asked if Bryan had ever stopped to think that if the earth suddenly stood still it would be converted into a molten mass of matter. Bryan replied no, he had never thought of it because he was too busy with more important things.

Darrow then switched to the story of the Flood and asked Bryan when it happened. In discussing the possible date and how it was arrived at, Darrow asked: "What do you think?" Bryan replied, "I do not think about things I don't think about." Darrow then said, "Do you think about things you do think about?" "Well, sometimes," was the answer. There was a burst of laughter at this, in which the judge joined.

As Darrow proceeded with his questions, the other prosecution attorneys realized that Bryan was beginning to look foolish. They interrupted and tried to stop the testimony, but, surprisingly, Judge Raulston permitted it to continue. Both Bryan and Darrow were getting angry, and some of the exchanges became acrimonious and even insulting. Soon they were shaking their fists at each other. Two red spots appeared on Bryan's cheeks, and his eyes glared with anger. Through it all the audience groaned or cheered as points were scored.

After another long wrangle over dates, Bryan stated that according to the Bible, Creation took place in 4004 B.C. or about six thousand years ago. But, said Darrow, there are civilizations that we know are older than that—the Chinese civilization goes back six or seven thousand years and the Egyptian even further. Impossible, retorted Bryan, they could not go back beyond Creation, six thousand years ago, no matter what any scientific man might say.

Toward the end of that long, hot afternoon Darrow questioned Bryan about the six days of Creation. It was here that Bryan—suddenly and inexplicably—"betrayed" his most zealous followers by saying he did not think the term "day" necessarily meant a day of twenty-four hours. He thought it meant a period, rather than a literal day, and that Creation could have gone on for a million years. Six days or six years or six million years or six hundred million years—"I do not think it important," said Bryan, "whether we believe one or the other."

The fundamentalists in the audience were horrified. From Bryan such a statement was a disastrous admission. If a Biblical day could be construed as a period of thousands of years, what happened to the literal interpretation of the Bible? At that moment Bryan was lost. Perhaps he did not mean to say it, perhaps he was goaded into it by Darrow's relentless insistence upon precise answers. Throughout the questioning, Bryan had tried to avoid exact statements while Darrow had sought tenaciously to pin him down. As Darrow persisted, Bryan became notice-ably less assured.

A few more questions were asked; a few more insults exchanged. Then a last outburst from Bryan: "The only purpose Mr. Darrow has is to slur at the Bible . . ." "I object to that," cried Darrow. "I am examining you on your fool ideas that no intelligent Christian on earth be-lieves." At this, the judge banged down his gavel and ad-journed the court.

Darrow's supporters leaped to the platform and milled around him enthusiastically. Many followed him home. Very few people, even among his own partisans, ap-proached Bryan, who stood wearily apart. The funda-mentalists turned away from him. He had let them down.

The next morning, rain forced the trial back inside. Dar-row had more questions to ask of Bryan, but the judge refused to allow them. He felt he had made a serious error in allowing Bryan to take the stand at all, and ordered the entire exchange removed from the trial record. Darrow re-plied that the defense was left with no case at all, since it had not been allowed to bring a single witness before the jury. He felt it was useless to continue and therefore asked the court to submit the case to the jurors without further delay and instruct them to find Scopes guilty.

Bryan was upset. He wanted to put Darrow on the stand and ask some questions of his own. More than that, he wanted to deliver a closing speech, which he had written some weeks before the trial even started. But the other prosecuting attorneys and the judge wanted to end the case. They ignored Bryan.

The judge instructed the jury to consider only whether Scopes had taught that man had descended from a lower order of animals. If he had, he was to be found guilty and fined from one hundred to five hundred dollars as provided by the law. If they felt that a hundred dollars was enough, they did not have to stipulate the fine, but could leave that to the judge.

Then Darrow asked the jury to bring in a unanimous verdict of guilty. That was the only way, he said, for the case to get to a higher court, and only a higher court could settle the question of whether the anti-evolution law was valid. Darrow wanted the case to be appealed to the Supreme Court so that the law could be declared unconstitutional.

The jury was out nine minutes before it returned with a verdict of guilty. Judge Raulston called Scopes to the bench and fined him a hundred dollars, then asked if he had anything to say.

"Your Honor," said Scopes, "I feel that I have been convicted of violating an unjust statute. I will continue to oppose this law. Any other action would violate my ideal of academic freedom—that is, to teach the truth as guaranteed in our Constitution."

The Dayton "monkey trial" was over.

Cordial farewells were taken. Darrow shook hands with the jurors, who expressed their disappointment at not being permitted to hear the scientific testimony. The courtroom audience, including many fundamentalists, came up to congratulate Darrow. He had won over the town. But the town had also won him over with its friendliness and hospitality.

After the trial ended, a dance was given in honor of Darrow, to which everyone was invited. He waltzed with the high school girls and joked with the boys.

Bryan, in the meantime, was busy revising and expanding the closing speech that he had been unable to give in court, so that it could be issued as a pamphlet. Four days after the trial ended, he drove two hundred miles in a blazing sun and delivered the speech twice before large audiences. The next day he led a Dayton church congregation in prayer, ate an enormous Sunday dinner, and then lay down for a nap. The strain of the trial, the heat, and the mountains of food he had consumed were too much for him. He died in his sleep.

A year later, the case came up on appeal. The Tennessee Supreme Court could either declare the law unconstitutional or it could reject the appeal, in which event the case could be brought to the United States Supreme Court, which was what Darrow wanted. But the court did neither. Instead, it reversed the verdict on a technicality, saying that the fine had been improperly imposed by the judge. According to the law, the jury should have done this. In his instructions to the jury, Judge Raulston had erred in telling them to leave the fine to him. The case was therefore dismissed.

Darrow felt the Scopes trial had achieved its main purpose: it had awakened the country to the attack on public schools and exposed the attempts of religious zealots to control education in the United States. It discouraged the passage of similar laws in other states, and no further attempt was made to enforce the Tennessee law, though it remained on the books. In Kentucky, when someone proposed an anti-evolution act not long afterward, it was laughed out of existence by the proposal of a companion measure ruling that water should run uphill in that state.

Above all, it made people think, and that was one of Darrow's chief aims: to get people to use their minds, to question, to doubt, to examine.

As a result of the Scopes trial, too, curiosity about evolution increased. During the next two years Darrow gave many lectures on evolution in various parts of the country. In 1931 a documentary motion picture on evolution was released, with Darrow as one of the narrators. It received good press notices, even in Tennessee.

22

---◆---

Race Conflict

After the Dayton trial, Darrow was bombarded with mail.
The letters, which continued to arrive for years, included
many threatening ones from cranks and fanatics who took
issue with his stand on evolution. Some, however, were
from devoutly religious well-wishers, begging him to repent
his sins before it was too late and telling him of prayer
groups which had been organized on his behalf. It was
impossible for him to read, still less to answer, all of them.
Occasionally he would gather a group of friends, and they
would go through a pile of letters together, reading aloud
the wildest or the most moving.

Scarcely had the excitement of the Dayton trial died
down when Darrow was drawn into his next important
case. This dealt with still another difficult and tragically
entangled area of American life, race relations.

In September, 1925, Dr. Ossian Sweet, a colored physician, moved into a house he had bought in Detroit. Dr. Sweet had worked his way through school and medical college and, after practicing in Detroit for a while, had gone abroad for advanced study in Vienna and Paris. Then he and his young wife and baby returned to Detroit.

He resumed his practice and in less than a year had made enough money to buy a house. The housing problem for Negroes in Detroit was acute. In 1915 Henry Ford introduced in Detroit the world's first assembly line and offered workers the unheard-of sum of five dollars a day. Shortly afterward, the First World War stepped up the need for cars and trucks. As a result Detroit soon became the automotive capital of the world, and thousands of workers moved into the city, especially from the South. Negroes alone, only a part of the Southern influx, increased from about seven thousand to seventy thousand in a dozen years.

The migration from the South had two unhappy results: first, the whites, mostly poor, unskilled labor, brought their racial prejudices with them; and, second, the Negroes found it almost impossible to get adequate housing in the overcrowded city. When they tried to move into white areas, they met with increasing antagonism.

In 1925 a series of attacks took place upon Negroes who tried to move into white neighborhoods. Their houses were damaged or destroyed, their lives threatened by white mobs. Even Negroes who had been living quietly in white streets were forced to move by the threat of violence.

Dr. Sweet was willing to pay a substantial amount for a decent house. The only one he could find was in an all-white neighborhood. He made it a point to visit the house several times and sit on the porch to give his future neighbors a good chance to look at him. If there were going to be any objection, he wanted it expressed before buying the house. "If I had known," he was to say later, "how bitter that neighborhood was going to be, I wouldn't have taken that house as a gift."

But no objections were raised, so he bought the house and, in September, moved in with his wife and two brothers, Henry and Otis. Otis was a dentist, Henry a senior at college who planned to go on to law school. The first night a crowd gathered in front of the house. The Sweets kept their lights off, fearful of provoking aggressive action. The mob hung around till about three in the morning, then drifted away. The Sweets felt relieved, resentful, and yet at the same time uneasy. Nevertheless, they decided to stay. This was their home, and they had the right to live in it.

The next day several friends came over to help fix up the new house. There were also present a hired man and Dr. Sweet's chauffeur. The Sweets' baby had been left with her grandmother during the confusion of moving.

As Mrs. Sweet was preparing dinner, Henry called out, "My God, look at the people!" A menacing crowd had gathered outside, and as Mrs. Sweet and the others joined Henry at the windows, stones began to fly. Just then a taxi drew up with Otis Sweet and a friend, and the two men had to race to the house through a hail of rocks. *"Get 'em!"* yelled the crowd. The house was now surrounded by a shrieking mob, and the Sweet brothers, who had grown up in the South where they had witnessed lynchings, were terrified. "I realized," said Dr. Sweet later, "that I was facing the same mob that had hounded my people throughout its history."

The besieged inmates put out the lights and drew down the shades. Dr. Sweet had brought in arms in anticipation of trouble. During the next few minutes the scene turned into a riot. Windows were broken, and Dr. Sweet was cut by flying glass. Then shots rang out, though from what direction it was impossible to tell.

A group of policemen, who had been standing by doing nothing while the crowd gathered, entered the house and arrested the occupants. The Sweets and their friends were taken in a patrol wagon to police headquarters where they learned, for the first time, that a white man had been killed during the shooting. They were charged with first-degree murder. Permission to telephone a lawyer was refused. When Mrs. Sweet's mother discovered what had happened, she called lawyers, but they were not allowed to see the prisoners. Writs of habeas corpus were secured, but the prosecutor's office still refused to produce the prisoners.

The National Association for the Advancement of Colored People heard about the incident and offered to handle the case. They asked Clarence Darrow to head the defense. He was in New York at the time, visiting Arthur Garfield Hays, who was to join the defense staff. The committee called upon Darrow at Hays's home. It consisted of Arthur Spingarn and Charles H. Studin, both lawyers, James Weldon Johnson, the Negro poet, and Walter White, an officer of the association. Spingarn, a black-haired, swarthy-faced man, described the Sweet affair to Darrow, who listened with great sympathy. "I fully understand the problems of your race," began Darrow. "But I am not a Negro," replied Spingarn. Darrow turned to Studin and said, *"You* understand what I mean." Studin said he was not a Negro either. "Well," said Darrow, turning to blond-haired, blue-eyed Walter White, "I won't make that mistake with you." "But I am a Negro," replied White.

Darrow went through his usual reasons for refusing to try the case: he was tired; he was growing old; he could not fight any more. But even as he spoke, he knew he would accept. To Darrow himself the color of a man's skin was irrelevant. But he knew that large numbers of Americans did not share this view and that in his fight for equality the Negro needed all the help he could get.

The first trial of the Sweets and their friends began at the end of October, 1925. The defense wanted to show that the eleven people on trial had exercised their legal right of self-defense. The prosecution claimed that there had been no need for self-defense, that the street had been quiet and peaceful that evening, with just a few people about on their usual affairs—going to the grocery, chatting with their neighbors, sitting on their porches enjoying the air. The shots had suddenly come from the Sweet house for no reason at all, killing an innocent bystander. It was a deliberate conspiracy to murder, said the prosecution, done without provocation and all the more unwarranted because extra policemen had been sent into the neighborhood that night to prevent trouble.

The state produced one witness after another, all of whom testified that there had been no crowd and no disturbance, no excitement of any kind that night. Darrow sat quietly through their statements, doing a crossword puzzle. These had just appeared in America, and Darrow was fascinated by them. He always kept some with him, together with a supply of pencils, and worked on them everywhere, in court, on trains, during lunch, at his office desk between periods of work.

When it came time for cross-examination of the witnesses, he put aside his puzzle, rose to his feet, and then, through patient questioning, drew a completely different picture of what happened. He would chat casually with the witness, put him at his ease, and ask questions that seemed harmless or innocuous. But by the time Darrow was through, about seventy witnesses had made it clear that a large crowd was present and that violence had been used against the Sweets. When one witness said pebbles had been thrown, Darrow asked him to indicate the size of the pebbles from a group of stones and pieces of cement that had been taken out of the Sweets' yard. The witness pointed to one about two inches in diameter. Darrow picked it up and started to hand it to the witness, but dropped it just before giving it to him. There was a loud crash—just as there must have been when the "pebble" went through the Sweets' window.

Even more important were the admissions drawn by Darrow that the white residents of the area had formed a "Water Works Improvement Association" for the sole purpose of keeping colored residents out of the neighborhood. If there had been any conspiracy, said Darrow, it was of the whites against the Sweets, not the other way around.

To help the jury imagine how that night must have seemed to the defendants, Darrow put Dr. Sweet on the stand and had him tell the story of the Negro in America, the mistreatment, the violence, the race riots which Dr. Sweet had seen with his own eyes.

In his address to the jury, Darrow continued with this revelation of the facts beneath the facts. He did not deny that shots were fired from the house but outlined in vivid detail the events and emotions that explained why they were fired.

The judge in the case, Frank Murphy, was fair and impartial, the most understanding man Darrow had ever seen on the bench. In his instructions to the jury, Judge Murphy made it clear that every man, colored or white, has the right to defend himself if his life or property is in danger.

The jury argued for forty-six hours without reaching a decision. The judge declared a mistrial and discharged them. The defense asked that their clients be released on bail—with the exception of Mrs. Sweet, all of them had been in jail ever since that night—and that each defendant be tried separately.

Of all the men, only young Henry Sweet had actually said he fired a gun. He had thought, when questioned the first night, that if he admitted the shooting the others would be released. As it turned out, the fatal bullet had not been fired from the gun he used. He was, however, selected as the first one to be tried separately, some five months after the original trial.

The second trial, with Henry Sweet as defendant, followed much the same course as the first, but Darrow's closing plea was even more eloquent in this second trial. It lasted seven hours. Again he did not deny that shots were fired from inside the house. But, "I do not care," he said. There were bigger issues than who fired the fatal bullet. These were the right to defend one's home and life and whether the Negro citizen was to be allowed to share that right.

The central issue was prejudice. At the very beginning of his address Darrow said that if the case had been reversed and eleven white men had defended their home against a colored mob, nobody would have dreamed of arresting them. Prejudice was something rarely, if ever, mentioned openly in trials of this sort, yet Darrow insisted over and over again that the case was not one of murder, but of bias. We are all prejudiced, he said, against other people's color, religion, politics, looks, dress. What he wanted to do was persuade the jury, as responsible citizens of a democracy, to step out of their prejudice, get inside the minds of colored people, and understand how they felt when the mob was attacking. Do you know what it means to be colored? he asked. And in a remarkable passage, Darrow virtually transformed his white listeners into Negroes, making them feel and suffer and understand the Negro's plight. The life of the Negro, he concluded, has been one of tragedy, injustice, and oppression. "The law has made him equal, but man has not."

The jury brought in a verdict of not guilty. The charges against the other defendants were dropped. But the Sweets never returned to their new house. Between the first and second trials, an attempt was made to burn it down. The house was boarded up and remained empty for a long time.

Today both white and colored families live on the street where Dr. Sweet and his family went through their painful ordeal.

23

---◆---

Hawaii: The Massie Case

In April, 1927, a banquet was given at the Palmer House in Chicago to celebrate Clarence Darrow's seventieth birthday. Twelve hundred men and women attended. One speaker after another praised Darrow for his defense of truth and humanity. A marble bust of Darrow was unveiled and presented to him.

At last Darrow himself rose and said: "Well, folks, I am the fellow that all the talking has been about. You have heard the speeches, you have seen the monument unveiled, and now the corpse will say a few words."

He spoke of his increasing sense of the futility of life. There is no plan, he said, no purpose, nothing except "a dream of freedom." As he spoke, however, he revealed to his audience a man whose life had been filled with purpose. "I have been fighting for the right of man to live and think and breathe and be unafraid. . . . All I want more of life is a greater capacity for kindness, forgiveness, and understanding."

At seventy, Darrow was tired. He had practiced law almost fifty years and had handled more than two thousand cases. In the summer following his birthday celebration, his health began to fail. Ruby insisted that he take time off for an extended rest. They went to Europe and stayed till late in the year, traveling in Italy, Germany, France, and around the Mediterranean, a region Darrow was especially fond of.

Soon after his return, while he was in New York, a committee came to his hotel to ask his help. Two men had been stabbed while marching in a fascist parade wearing the full uniform of Mussolini's fascist supporters in Italy. Agents of Mussolini came to New York and worked with the city's police department, carrying out a series of raids against anti-fascist newspaper offices and private homes. Several men were arrested, and two, Calogero Greco and Donato Carillo, were charged with the stabbing on very flimsy evidence. A defense committee was formed, and Darrow was asked to take the case.

"No," said Darrow, "I'm tired, I want to rest. . . . " Among those on the committee was Greco's brother. As Darrow continued to refuse, Philippo Greco began to weep. Darrow looked at him impatiently, then said, "All right— all right—I'll take the case. For God's sake, stop crying." The trial began in December and lasted three weeks. In his address to the jury, Darrow included an attack upon fascism. On Christmas Eve, the jury brought in a verdict of not guilty, and the defendants, to Darrow's embarrassment, rushed over and kissed his hands.

In 1928 Paul Darrow sold the gas plant which was still being operated in Colorado. Darrow made a good profit from the sale and promptly invested it in stocks. At last, he thought, he would be able to retire permanently. Not long afterward, early in 1929, he had trouble with his heart. Now he had no choice; he had to stop working.

He and Ruby left for a year in Europe. They had been abroad many times before, but never for so long. They spent two months in Montreux, on the shore of Lake Geneva in Switzerland. Here he began to write his autobiography.

At the end of the summer they left for a motor trip through England, Scotland, Wales, the Isle of Wight, and Ireland. Then they went south to the French Riviera to spend the winter at Cannes. It was beautiful and serene, and Darrow settled down to work again on his autobiography, later published as *The Story of My Life*. Clarence wrote in a penciled scrawl, which Ruby patiently deciphered, corrected, and typed.

When they were not working, the Darrows strolled along the Mediterranean or visited old friends, like the American writer and diplomat Brand Whitlock who had settled permanently in Europe, and new ones, like the English writers Somerset Maugham and H. G. Wells. Wells shared Darrow's love of crossword puzzles; they played time-limit games, each working at his own copy of the same puzzle to see who could finish first.

To Darrow, Europe was a place where "everyone seemed to enjoy joy; where pleasure carried with it no suggestion of wickedness." He felt that America was still under the dreary influence of the early Puritans who associated pleasure with sin and saw life as a matter of grim duty. The Europeans, on the contrary, had learned the art of living. "In Europe," said Darrow, "no one is afraid to enjoy life in his own way." There was little of the excessive concentration on work and moneymaking that he found in America. He liked the long two-hour recess for lunch; he liked the sidewalk cafés where friends could relax over a bottle of wine. He liked the casual gaiety which he missed at home.

Though Darrow was a confirmed pessimist, brooding over the tribulations and injustices of a badly ordered world, he was also a confirmed pleasure seeker. "I am a hedonist," he used to say, "and have contempt for anyone who isn't."

Late in 1929, while he was still in Europe, the stock market crashed. Most of Darrow's holdings were lost. When he returned home to look into his affairs, he discovered that the investment income on which he had planned to retire had almost disappeared.

He wrote later that what cushioned the shock was his lifelong pessimism. Since he was always prepared for the worst, he was never too upset when it happened, unlike the optimist who, living in the clouds, had a long way to fall when the clouds parted and he crashed to earth.

He often spoke about the consolations of pessimism, and liked to quote one of his favorite poets, A. E. Housman, who said that since

> *Luck's a chance, but trouble's sure,*
> *I'd face it as a wise man would,*
> *And train for ill and not for good.*

To have the consolations of pessimism was not enough, however. Darrow was now, at seventy-two, faced all over again with the problem of earning a living. He did not want to go back to law. After his return from Europe, he never went back to the routine of a regular practice, though he did take an occasional case.

He turned again, but more seriously, to lecturing and debating. In earlier years these had been diversions, something to do in the time left over from his legal work or between big cases. Now they became his chief occupation and principal source of income. He spent the next two years traveling back and forth over the country, speaking in practically all the large cities, visiting every state except, for some reason he could never explain, Oklahoma.

Many of his debates centered about religion. He went on several long tours during which, in each city, he took part in a four-man discussion with local clergymen or spokesmen for the Protestant, Catholic, and Jewish faiths. Darrow took the agnostic view; he was the man with the questions the others tried to answer. Or as he put it, "I alone represented the unrighteous, although I frequently had some consolation, and sometimes aid, from the rabbi." He could not accept any of the religious views of the universe, and was particularly unable to believe in an afterlife. Nobody had ever given him convincing proof of a future life, "and I don't know that I would want it if there were."

Even though his own life had contained great happiness, Darrow had seen so much hopeless despair in the lives of his clients, so much injustice and unreason in the world that he found himself unable to believe in a divinely ordered pattern. Nor could he find such a design in nature, which to him appeared cruel and capricious. Wherever he looked, he saw animals devouring each other or perishing in great natural disasters. "There is no place in the woods or air or sea where all life is not a carnage of death in terror and agony." What design or purpose is there, he asked, in earthquakes that wipe out whole populations, in plagues of insects who devour the food laboriously raised by farmers, in microbes that bring a man to a painful death? And what of wars, in which men slaughter each other while calling on their God for help? He could not reconcile such disasters "with the idea that back of the universe is a Supreme Being, all merciful and kind. . . . Whichever way man may look upon the earth, he is oppressed with the suffering incident to life. It would almost seem as though the earth had been created with malignity and hatred."

He was convinced that life was a tragedy and that anything—good or bad—could happen to anyone at any time by the merest chance. Man did not have the slightest control over his destiny. He used to laugh at the poem by William Ernest Henley which contained the lines,

I am the master of my fate,
I am the captain of my soul.

"A fine captain," said Darrow. "Why, man isn't even a deckhand on a rudderless ship!"

In his autobiography he wrote: "We are like a body of shipwrecked sailors clutching to a raft and desperately engaged in holding on. . . . The best that we can do is to be kindly and helpful toward our friends and fellow passengers who are clinging to the same speck of dirt while we are drifting side by side to our common doom."

Fortunately for both Darrow and his close associates, this dark view of life was relieved by his sense of humor. He saw a large part of life as a joke, and he always loved a joke. Even at his most cynical, he was good-humored and witty in his dissection of human folly. And for all his insistence that life was utterly futile, he wanted to go on living as long and as happily as he could. "This living business is a habit," he once said to a friend. "I'm used to it now, sort of got the hang of it, and on a pleasant day like this, I want to go on living."

His friends suspected that he enjoyed his pessimism. "He liked to sit around and talk by the hour, saying gloomier and gloomier things and having a better and better time." And on his seventy-sixth birthday he said jovially, "Congratulate me on not having to stay in this fool world much longer."

Many of his religious opponents insisted that though Darrow argued for agnosticism, he practiced Christianity in his own life. Dr. Clarence True Wilson, a Methodist minister who debated with Darrow more than forty times, said, "If kindliness and brotherliness, square dealing, fair treatment, doing unto others as you would have them do unto you are Christian traits, then Darrow had the Christian characteristics without a Christian creed." Dr. Wilson had "abhorred" Darrow before meeting him. Darrow had championed people whom Wilson regarded as menaces to society. But at their first meeting Wilson saw "the face of one of the most genial, lovable, friendly, frank men our nation ever produced." Though they remained worlds apart in their views, the devout and believing Wilson developed a warm affection and admiration for the agnostic Darrow. There were many other deeply religious men who felt that Darrow, with his boundless compassion, was closer to God and a more perfect Christian than many of those who criticized his lack of religion.

Darrow enjoyed the religious debates. Before each one the four antagonists would meet at breakfast and discuss the program. After the debate they would go to someone's home for hours of conversation with the local elite.

Audiences would start out distrusting or disliking the "infidel" Darrow. But he would win them over just as he had won over judges and juries in the courtroom. By the end of the evening his listeners loved him. Many who had despised his views began to worry about him and sent letters saying they felt it their duty to rescue him from eternal doom. Some wrote original prayers for him, or set aside definite hours during the day when they prayed for his soul. Religious books, tracts, pamphlets, copies of the Bible came in such numbers that he scarcely had time to unwrap and examine them.

It was a pleasant interlude in his life. His son Paul now lived only a block away from his father's apartment, and Darrow took great delight in the frequent company of his three young granddaughters. He saw a good deal, too, of his sister Jennie, a schoolteacher, and his brother Herman, a proofreader, the two youngest of all the Darrow brothers and sisters. With Clarence they were the only ones still alive of Amirus' children. There were, however, a host of nieces and nephews who often gathered at the Darrow home.

His principal burden at this time was the daily mail. In addition to letters concerned with his salvation, there were requests for money, assistance, or advice. Young people asked about problems connected with becoming lawyers; people in legal difficulties asked for his aid; would-be writers sent their manuscripts for reading and even marketing. Almost every day brought at least one letter from someone in jail, pleading for help or sympathy.

The invitations and pleas to try cases never ceased. He refused the great majority of these, but every now and then a particular case would appeal to him, and he would return briefly to the legal arena.

In 1931 it seemed, for a moment, that he would return into the glare of publicity that had surrounded his major trials. The National Association for the Advancement of Colored People asked him and Arthur Garfield Hays to defend the eight young Negroes in the Scottsboro case.

Darrow and Hays went to Birmingham, where the boys were being held, and discovered that a left-wing organization had already assumed charge. Their representative said he would be glad to have the assistance of Darrow and Hays but only under certain conditions.

Darrow tipped down his head and looked at the man over the top of his glasses. It was a long time, he replied, since anyone had presented him with conditions upon taking a case, but what were they? The conditions were that Darrow and Hays repudiate the NAACP and leave all tactics to the group in charge. Even if Darrow should feel that the tactics were unwise or harmful, he would have nothing to say about them. Darrow refused, saying his only responsibility must be to the defendants and to no one else. This was, in turn, refused. Darrow and Hays felt they could not work under such circumstances, and withdrew from the case.

They were accused of withdrawing out of fear of being associated with a radical group. The fact that Darrow had unhesitatingly defended the Communist Labor party members on trial after the First World War was ignored. Public antagonism had not prevented him from taking that case, though a good deal of the antagonism had rubbed off on him. In the Scottsboro case, he felt that the main issue, the defense of the accused, would be subordinated to political purposes. In the communist trial, Darrow had been concerned with legal rights, not with political propaganda. He would defend those rights in the face of any danger. But he would not use that defense as propaganda for any party.

In the spring of 1932, he accepted the last of his big cases. Like the Sweet affair, this involved racial tensions, to the point where the crime itself became less important than its social implications.

Mrs. Thalia Massie, the young wife of an American naval lieutenant stationed in Hawaii, had walked out of a party shortly before midnight. She had found the hot, noisy atmosphere uncomfortable and wanted fresh air; she had also quarreled with her husband. On her way home she was assaulted by five men who beat her severely, breaking her jaw in two places. Two of the men were Hawaiians, two Japanese, and one Chinese. The next day she identified four of the men. They were arrested and tried, but the jury, most of whom were natives, disagreed, and the four men were released on bail pending a new trial.

Hostility flared up between the white and nonwhite populations. Hawaii had been annexed by the United States in 1898, and relations were still sensitive. The whites felt that the native police and the district attorney's office had been deliberately slack in prosecuting the case. The nonwhites saw the trial as a symbol of oppression and raised large defense funds for the accused men. Malicious gossip was spread in an attempt to discredit the Massies' version of the affair. Feelings were further aggravated when one of the Hawaiians, a football star, played in the games held every Sunday and had his name headlined in Monday's sports pages.

Lieutenant Massie, distressed and infuriated by these events, came to the conclusion that the false rumors could not be stopped nor would any jury find the men guilty unless they confessed. He decided to take matters into his own hands and force them to admit their guilt. He seized one of the Japanese and beat him till he confessed. The man had photographs taken of the welts on his back, and Massie was told by his lawyer that the confession would not be admissible in court.

Massie then kidnapped Kahahawai, the Hawaiian leader of the group. He was helped in this by his wife's mother, Mrs. Fortescue, and by two sailors in his naval unit. Kahahawai was taken to Mrs. Fortescue's house where he admitted the attack. As he said, "Yeah, we done it," Lieutenant Massie, enraged, fired his service revolver and killed him.

Massie, Mrs. Fortescue, and the two sailors were arrested and charged with murder. Feeling on the islands now exploded. Racial lines were drawn: Kahahawai was set up as a martyr by one side and as a villain who deserved killing by the other. The agitation spread to the mainland.

The defense asked Darrow to take their case. He hesitated, with good reason. He was reaching seventy-five—his seventy-fifth birthday was spent in Honolulu, as it turned out—and did not know if he could stand the effort of traveling to Hawaii and the strain of a daily court routine. He had been retired for four years and was no longer certain that he still had enough vigor and alertness for a court battle. His friends urged him to take the case, especially since it meant a fee of twenty-five thousand dollars, and for all his lecture tours, the Darrows were still in need of money. He finally agreed, saying later that he had never been to Honolulu and wanted to see it. Perhaps an even stronger motive was that people had been saying Darrow was through as a lawyer, and "I wanted to show them that a man in his seventies was keener than a young person."

It soon became evident that Clarence Darrow was not only still "keener than a young person" but a good deal more effective just by the mere fact of his presence. The Hawaiian newspapers had been indifferent or unfriendly to the defendants. The most antagonistic of these changed its tone after Darrow entered the case because, said the editor, Darrow would not have taken it "unless he were convinced it was right in principle." During the preliminary hearings the defendants had been oppressed by the hostility of the court personnel and spectators, but with Darrow on the scene, a noticeable thaw set in. Mrs. Fortescue felt almost at once that the "human love" radiating from Darrow was replacing the hatred with understanding.

He went through the jury selection with his usual care and set the whole mood of his appeal to them with comments like these: "We can trust you, can't we?" or "We can rely upon you for a fair trial, can't we? I know we can."

He took no notes during the trial and made no apparent preparation for his final address. But the summation, which lasted four hours and twenty minutes, was as perfectly organized and cogent as if it had been carefully worked over and outlined in minute detail.

The courtroom was jammed with people who wanted to see and hear Clarence Darrow. Many had waited in line all night to be sure of getting into the courthouse when it opened in the morning. Some latecomers persuaded people to sell their places for as much as twenty-five dollars each. On the American mainland, thousands listened to the address broadcast over the radio directly from the courtroom.

Darrow based his plea entirely on the actions and emotions of the people concerned, not on legal technicalities or loopholes. The case, he said, illustrated "the effect of sorrow and mishap on human minds."

As he had done in the Sweet case, Darrow tried to get the jury to put themselves in the defendants' places, to imagine how they would have reacted under the same provocations. He did not deny the guilt of his clients. He freely admitted that they had indeed committed a crime and gave all the details. But he presented these details as the acts of people goaded into violence by extreme distress. Step by step he led the jury through the background of the crime, showing how the mental anguish of the defendants was built up.

Only at the very end of his address did he speak of the racial issue. He told the jury that he had deliberately avoided it because he wanted them to consider the case in human terms without regard to race or nationality. But even without emphasizing the racial tensions, he had his effect upon them. Admiral Yates Stirling, in charge of American naval forces in Hawaii, was impressed by the change in atmosphere created by Darrow's personality. He wrote in his memoirs: "Darrow, his coat hanging loosely about his bony frame, breathed kindliness and sympathy for all. The courtroom seemed pervaded with his gentle, old voice. Its soothing effect was miraculous to see. Slowly his voice was stamping out all bitterness."

Though Admiral Stirling saw Darrow as "an old man, gentle and human," Darrow showed no trace of age or weakness during his address. When he finished, however, and walked back to his seat, the marks of age and weariness could be seen on his lined face.

The judge gave his instructions to the jury, pointing out that regardless of the provocations, the defendants had nevertheless committed a crime. After two days of deliberation, the jury returned with a verdict of manslaughter but with a recommendation of leniency. The judge's explicit instructions had made it impossible for them to bring in a verdict of not guilty. The defendants were sentenced to ten years in jail.

There was an immediate public protest. In Washington, congressmen asked that full pardons be granted without delay. The governor of Hawaii summoned Darrow and his clients to his office where he announced that he would commute the sentence to one hour. The prisoners, with Darrow to keep them company, sat in the governor's palace for the next hour, and then were set free.

The island authorities made plans to retry the remaining men who had assaulted Mrs. Massie and asked Darrow to join the prosecution. He declined, saying that he had never prosecuted anyone and could not begin now. He had always been with the hunted, never the hunters.

He did something far better than help the prosecution. He persuaded them, and Mrs. Massie as well, to drop the case altogether and take no further action. Enough racial bitterness had been aroused; it would be best for everyone to forget the whole unhappy episode. "Questions of race," he had said at the end of his plea, "must be solved by understanding—not by force." A new trial would only make matters worse; it would not further the understanding and harmony he wanted to encourage. "I'd like to think I had done my small part to bring peace and justice to an Island wracked and worn by strife."

At his suggestion, therefore, the affair came to an end. With this accomplished, Darrow left Hawaii and, at the same time, left forever the courtrooms where for more than fifty years he had done his part to bring justice and peace to a world torn by strife, injustice, and intolerance.

24

Final Plea

Though Darrow was through with major court trials, he was not quite finished with public life.

In 1929 the stock market crash ended the big boom of the twenties and set off the great depression of the thirties. By the end of 1932, one of the darkest years in America's life, there were seventeen million unemployed. Poverty, starvation, hopeless misery, which had always existed to some degree among the working class, now spread to other sections of the population.

Millions who had rarely known economic insecurity lost their incomes and joined the ranks of the dispossessed. Every day more businesses failed, more banks closed their doors. Bread lines and soup kitchens became common sights. Unemployed men and women sold apples on street corners. Labor strife, never completely absent even during the prosperous twenties, erupted dramatically, particularly among textile workers and coal miners.

Tragic as these circumstances were, they tended in the long run to improve the conditions of labor. Since the 1890's, Clarence Darrow had struggled against the indifference of the public and the government toward the hardships endured by American workers. Now, in the great depression, bad working conditions became so acute that at last labor began to receive direct aid from the government. In 1932 the Norris-La Guardia Act was passed, granting workers the right to organize into unions and bargain collectively, and forbidding the use of the injunction as an antiunion or antistrike weapon. This was a decided victory for principles which Darrow had supported for over forty years.

In that same year Franklin Delano Roosevelt was elected President, and efforts toward recovery moved into high speed under the dynamic impetus of his New Deal. Immediate help was given to the unemployed in the form of outright relief funds and work projects. Longer-range benefits were provided by the Social Security Act, establishing unemployment insurance and old age pensions. The Wagner National Labor Relations Act, passed in 1935, strengthened the effect of the Norris-La Guardia Act. The government was now firmly behind labor's efforts to improve its conditions. Labor had been accepted as a full partner in the economic life of the nation.

Roosevelt realized, however, that protecting the rights of workingmen would mean little unless they had jobs. The economy had to be put back on its feet as soon as possible;

business had to be stimulated. To accomplish this, Roosevelt, a brilliant improviser when faced with an emergency, set up the National Recovery Administration, symbolized by a blue eagle. Under the NRA, industries were to set up codes establishing production quotas, regulating prices, and restricting ruinous competition. Labor's rights were safeguarded by the famous Section 7a which gave workers the right to organize and to negotiate wages and hours.

The NRA, an emergency measure hastily and improperly drafted, had serious faults. It violated the antitrust laws by permitting industries to establish monopoly practices; it protected big business at the expense of small. Small businessmen protested so loudly against the NRA that the New Deal leaders set up an impartial review board to study the act and its effects.

It was imperative that such a board be headed by a fair and impartial chairman. Senator Gerald Nye proposed Clarence Darrow; President Roosevelt and General Hugh S. Johnson, the administrator of the NRA, agreed.

So Clarence and Ruby went to Washington, a humming, stirring vortex of action, much of it confused, all of it vigorous and determined. Darrow reported to General Johnson, a blunt and bellicose army man ready to defend the NRA Blue Eagle to its last feather.

At their first interview Darrow said, "Supposing we find out the codes are not all right?" "Then you report to me," said Johnson, jabbing his chest with his thumb. "I am the big cheese here."

Darrow replied quietly that he did not think he would care to do that. He went directly to President Roosevelt and told him that to submit his findings to the head of the organization under investigation did not seem to him an impartial proceeding. Roosevelt agreed and made the Darrow Board, as it came to be called, responsible only to him.

For the next four months Darrow, now seventy-seven years old, worked up to fourteen hours a day. He studied thirty-four codes in detail, conducted almost sixty public hearings, looked into at least three thousand complaints. As the investigations proceeded, he realized that the NRA did indeed favor big business at the expense of small. At the end of three months he sent his first report to President Roosevelt. When Johnson heard of its adverse findings, he roared in outrage and gave the press a statement refuting Darrow's criticisms. Relations between the two men became strained, to say the least. Darrow wrote two more reports, blasting away at the errors of the NRA and recommending specific reforms. Johnson continued his vociferous objections. Newspapermen followed the disputes of these two colorful and independent personalities. One cartoonist showed Darrow and Johnson each hanging on to a foot of a distressed NRA Blue Eagle, with the caption, "A couple of lions making the eagle scream."

But Darrow was used to outspoken opponents and persisted in his charge that most of the NRA codes had been drawn up by big business, to its own advantage.

Early the following spring Darrow gave his final critical views to a senate investigating committee. Two months later the Supreme Court unanimously declared the NRA unconstitutional, and it was abandoned.

Many of its good features, particularly the sections protecting labor, were incorporated into other laws or agencies of the New Deal. The fair treatment of labor, for which Darrow had fought so long, was firmly established. Collective bargaining, minimum pay, maximum hours, the abolition of child labor, unemployment insurance, and old-age pensions—all these were accepted. Never again would American workingmen have to convince a hostile public or an indifferent Administration that these were legitimate rights.

Not all employers were ready to embrace the new era of industrial relations. There were still major strikes to come, like those in the steel and automobile industries later on in the 1930's. But by the end of the decade the powerful CIO—Congress of Industrial Organizations—had been established, and the new relationship between worker and employer was an accomplished fact. In the light of past labor history, it was an almost revolutionary fact.

The automobile strike introduced a new labor weapon, the sit-down. Instead of leaving their factories, the men remained at their workbenches, making it impossible for strikebreakers to take their places. It was denounced as a violation of private property rights, but for the next two years union after union "sat down." The workers sang, "When the boss won't talk, don't take a walk, Sit down! Sit down!"

Darrow did not approve of the sit-down technique. He felt the workers were able to gain their ends peacefully through the legal channels now open to them. "I sympathize with their objectives," he said during an interview, "but I don't like their methods. I'm enough of a lawyer for that. It pays to get what you want by legal methods. It makes the pact more binding, leaves less bitterness to be forgotten."

Darrow's long support and friendship for organized labor did not cloud his judgment when he thought labor was wrong. No party, group, or viewpoint could ever command his uncritical allegiance. He remained his own man. The CIO itself soon abandoned sit-down strikes.

With his work on the NRA Review Board, Darrow had performed his last public service for "the small fellow." It was time to rest, and he badly needed rest. He returned to Chicago and took up his old routine once more, though from this time on it slowed perceptibly. His heart began to give him more trouble; he had to content himself with doing less. But he continued to do some writing, see friends, read voluminously, even travel a little. He made a nostalgic trip to Kinsman, visiting the few friends who were left and looking once more at his old home and his boyhood playgrounds.

One of his last trips was to Stateville Prison to visit Nathan Leopold. Loeb had been killed in a prison fight the year before. Whenever Darrow could manage it, he had gone to see them and between visits had sent encouraging letters. He felt it was a lawyer's responsibility to give whatever help he could, beyond the required legal services. Leopold has given a moving and perceptive client's-eye view of his attorney. He felt that the keynote of Darrow's "many-faceted character" was kindliness. "He knew sor-

row and trouble intimately; his instantaneous reaction toward people—especially people in trouble—was the welling
forth of that tremendous, instinctive kindliness and sympathy." Though Darrow abhorred many human actions
and hated "cruelty, narrow-mindedness, or obstinate stu-
pidity," he never hated the individuals who manifested
these traits. He despised the quality, never the man. On
that last visit, Darrow looked feeble. "The mark of death
was on his face. But age and illness had not dimmed that
piercing inner light. His wisdom, his kindliness, his understanding love of his fellow man shone out as brilliantly on
this last day I saw him as it had on the first."

On his eightieth birthday a reporter came to interview
him. "Do you think I look eighty years old?" Darrow
asked. The reporter looked at the face which had always
been lined, at the brow which had always jutted out over
the deep-set blue eyes, at the compassionate expression
that had always been there. He replied: "Mr. Darrow, you
have always looked eighty years old."

He spent most of his last year sitting in his favorite chair
reading, or standing at the bay window of his apartment
looking out over what he called "the prettiest view on
earth." It was the view looking out over Jackson Park. The
spot he loved most in the park was a little bridge over the
lagoon. He used to take one of his granddaughters there
when she was a child to watch the squirrels. On the hun-
dredth anniversary of his birthday, two decades later, the
citizens of Chicago would hold a day-long celebration, and
as part of it they would name the bridge the "Clarence
Darrow Memorial Bridge."

Toward the end of the year he was confined to bed. On May 13, 1938, just before his eighty-first birthday, he died.

The next day he lay in state, while hundreds of people filed past. On the following day he was moved to the chapel at the University of Chicago where a memorial service was held. From all over the city there came friends, admirers, former clients, law students, legal colleagues, city and labor leaders, scientists from the University of Chicago, and the poor and unfortunate whom he had helped. Those who could not get into the crowded chapel stood outside in a pouring rain. Judge William H. Holly, who had once been Darrow's law partner, delivered an address.

"Thousands of lives," he said, "were made richer and happier because Clarence Darrow lived. . . . His great abilities were given freely to the cause of human liberty and for the succor of the weak and the unfortunate."

Clarence Darrow had traveled a long way from his childhood in Kinsman. But was he so far removed from that starting point? He had, after all, followed in the direct line of his father Amirus, the village skeptic who had insisted upon thinking for himself and had assumed as his own the struggles of the oppressed. Amirus Darrow, the abolitionist, had helped fleeing slaves on their way to freedom; his son had fought for the civic rights and true equality of the Negro. Amirus had argued for the rights of workers and had himself represented the small artisan; his son, at great cost, had defended labor organizers, worked for collective bargaining, and exposed discrimination against small businessmen.

Amirus Darrow had acted out in his own life the belief that every man must be involved in humanity; his son had taken active steps to improve and protect the condition of his fellow men. The love of knowledge, the fearless search for truth, the application of reason and tolerance to the solution of human conflicts—these were the cornerstones of life for Amirus; they were no less so for Clarence.

Darrow put his ideas to work in the courtroom where he pioneered in broadening the narrow or vengeful treatment of crime into the full consideration of the criminal as a human being. He awakened society to its own responsibility in causing crime and dramatized the importance of psychiatric testimony in criminal cases. His ideals of individual liberty and freedom of speech were translated into realities by his defense of unpopular causes.

The prime motive of his nature was compassion. But he was also oppressed by an awareness of human imperfection, and so his feeling for humanity was clouded by sorrow. His high dreams for the human race were troubled by his brooding conviction that they could never be realized. Though he called himself a pessimist with hope, he was also a dreamer with skepticism.

This produced a constant inner anguish, relieved, however, by his sense of humor and his untrammeled enjoyment of life's pleasures. His mind was complex and resourceful, yet he was at the same time the essence of unaffected simplicity.

He was a giant of his own age and, in courage, spirit, and crusading energy, an inspiration to ours.

Selected Bibliography

Adamic, Louis. *Dynamite, The Story of Class Violence in America.* New York: The Viking Press, 1934 (revised edition).

Adelman, Abram E. "Clarence Darrow—'Take Him for All in All,' " *Age of Reason Magazine,* October 1955, pp. 1–4.

Baillie, Hugh. *High Tension.* New York: Harper & Brothers, 1959.

Barnard, Harry. *Eagle Forgotten, The Life of John Peter Altgeld.** Indianapolis: The Bobbs-Merrill Company, Inc., 1938.

Bennema, J. G. "Clarence Darrow's Birthday Party," *The International Engineer,* May 1927, pp. 391–392.

Busch, Francis X. *Prisoners at the Bar.** Indianapolis: The Bobbs-Merrill Company, Inc., 1952. William D. Haywood case, pp. 15–50; Loeb-Leopold case, pp. 145–199.

Cohen, Alfred; Chisholm, Joe. *"Take the Witness!"* New York: Frederick A. Stokes Company, 1934.

Crandall, Allen. *The Man from Kinsman.* Sterling, Colorado: Published by the author, 1933.

Darrow, Clarence. *Crime, Its Cause and Treatment.* New York: Thomas Y. Crowell Company, 1922.

―――. *An Eye for an Eye.*† New York: Fox, Duffield & Company, 1905.

―――. *Farmington.*† Chicago: A. C. McClurg & Co., 1904.

* Available in paperback reprints.
† Available in Big Blue Books, Haldeman-Julius Publications, Girard, Kansas.

Darrow, Clarence (with Wallace Rice). *Infidels and Heretics.* Boston: The Stratford Company, 1929.

————. *A Persian Pearl and Other Essays.* East Aurora, New York: Roycroft Press, 1899. Chicago: C. L. Ricketts, 1902.

———— (with Victor S. Yarros). *The Prohibition Mania.* New York: Boni & Liveright, 1927.

————. *Resist Not Evil.*† Chicago: Charles H. Kerr, 1902.

————. *The Story of My Life.** New York: Charles Scribner's Sons, 1932.

Darrow, Clarence. Articles, pamphlets, court addresses, short stories, debates. At least ninety of these were published. The most important can be found, in whole or part, in the two collections by Arthur and Lila Weinberg. (See below, under Weinberg.) Some are still available in the "Little Blue Books" published by the Haldeman-Julius Company, Girard, Kansas. Excerpts in the text from these shorter works (aside from courtroom material) come mainly from *The Open Shop,* The Hammersmark Publishing Company, 1904 (also Haldeman-Julius Little Blue Book No. 1425), and "Attorney for the Defense," *Esquire,* May 1936, pp. 36–37, 211–213.

"Darrow: Tender-Hearted Cynic and Fixture of American Law," *News-Week,* May 19, 1934, p. 14.

Decker, Mary Bell. "The Man Clarence Darrow," *The University Review* (University of Kansas City), Summer 1938, pp. 238–242.

Dedmon, Emmett. *Fabulous Chicago.* New York: Random House, 1953.

Fortescue, Mrs. Granville. "The Honolulu Martyrdom," *Liberty,* July 30, August 6, August 13, 1932.

Garland, Hamlin. *Companions on the Trail.* New York: The Macmillan Company, 1931.

Giesler, Jerry. *The Jerry Giesler Story* as told to Pete Martin. New York: Simon and Schuster, 1960.

Ginger, Ray. *Altgeld's America.* New York: Funk & Wagnalls Company, 1958.

————. *The Bending Cross.* New Brunswick: Rutgers University Press, 1949.

————. "Clarence Seward Darrow, 1857–1938," *The Antioch Review*, Spring 1953, pp. 52–66.

————. *Six Days or Forever?** Boston: Beacon Press, 1958.

Goldman, Eric F. *Rendezvous With Destiny.** New York: Alfred A. Knopf, Inc., 1952.

Gompers, Samuel. *Seventy Years of Life and Labor*. Rev. and ed. by Philip Taft and John A. Sessions. New York: E. P. Dutton & Co., Inc., 1957.

Grebstein, Sheldon Norman, ed. *Monkey Trial*. Boston: Houghton Mifflin Company, 1960.

Haldeman-Julius, Marcet. *Clarence Darrow's Two Great Trials*. Girard, Kansas: Haldeman-Julius Company, 1927. Scopes trial, pp. 3–25; Sweet case, pp. 27–74.

Harrison, Charles Yale. *Clarence Darrow*. New York: Jonathan Cape & Harrison Smith, 1931.

Hays, Arthur Garfield. *Let Freedom Ring*. New York: Liveright Publishing Corporation, 1937. Scopes trial, pp. 25–89; Sweet case, pp. 195–233.

————. *Trial by Prejudice*. New York: Covici, Friede, 1933.

Holly, William H. "Funeral Address," *Unity*, May 16, 1938, pp. 86–87.

Kinney, Charlotte. "Clarence Darrow As He Is," *Psychology*, August 1932, pp. 15–17, 46–47.

Kunstler, William M. *The Case for Courage*. New York: William Morrow and Company, 1962.

Leopold, Nathan F., Jr. *Life plus 99 Years*. Garden City, New York: Doubleday & Company, Inc., 1958.

Maloney, Martin. "The Forensic Speaking of Clarence Darrow," *Speech Monographs*, 1947, pp. 110–126.

Martin, John Bartlow. "Murder on His Conscience," *Saturday Evening Post*, April 2, April 9, April 16, April 23, 1955.

Mason, Lowell B. "Darrow vs. Johnson," *North American Review*, December 1934, pp. 524–532.

Masters, Edgar Lee. *Across Spoon River*. New York: Farrar & Rinehart, Inc., 1936.

Mordell, Albert. *Clarence Darrow, Eugene V. Debs and Haldeman-Julius*. Girard, Kansas: Haldeman-Julius Publications, 1950.

Nathan, George Jean. *The Intimate Notebooks of George Jean Nathan.* New York: Alfred A. Knopf, Inc., 1932, pp. 80–94.

Owen, Russell. "Darrow—A Pessimist With Hope—Is Eighty," *The New York Times Magazine,* April 18, 1937, p. 5.

Rahskoph, Horace G. "The Speaking of Clarence Darrow," *American Public Address,* Loren Reid, ed. Columbia: University of Missouri Press, 1961, pp. 27–53.

Ravitz, Abe C. *Clarence Darrow and the American Literary Tradition.* Cleveland: The Press of Western Reserve University, 1962.

————; Primm, James N. *The Haywood Case.* San Francisco: Chandler Publishing Company, 1963.

St. Johns, Adela Rogers. *Final Verdict.* Garden City, New York: Doubleday & Company, Inc., 1962.

Steffens, Lincoln. *The Autobiography of Lincoln Steffens.* New York: Harcourt, Brace and Company, Inc., 1931.

Stirling, Yates. *Sea Duty.* New York: G. P. Putnam's Sons, 1939.

Stone, Irving. *Clarence Darrow for the Defense.* Garden City, New York: Doubleday & Company, Inc., 1941.

Unity, May 16, 1938. Contains group of articles on Clarence Darrow by various authors.

Weinberg, Arthur, ed. *Attorney for the Damned.* New York: Simon and Schuster, 1957.

————. "Clarence Darrow's Son Says: 'I Remember Father,' " *Chicago Tribune Magazine,* May 6, 1956, p. 19.

Weinberg, Arthur and Lila, eds. *Clarence Darrow, Verdicts Out of Court.* Chicago: Quadrangle Books, 1963.

Werner, M. R. *Bryan.* New York: Harcourt, Brace and Company, 1929.

Whitehead, George G. *Clarence Darrow—The Big Minority Man.* Girard, Kansas: Haldeman-Julius Little Blue Book No. 1464, no date. Reprinted from *Debunker,* May 1929.

"Who Is This Man Darrow?" *Current Literature,* August 1907, pp. 157–159.

Wilson, Clarence True. "Darrow, Friendly Enemy," *Forum,* July 1938, pp. 12–16.

Yarros, Victor. *My 11 Years With Clarence Darrow.* Girard, Kansas: Haldeman-Julius Publications, 1950.

Index

273

About the Author

Miriam Gurko is deeply interested in both history and literature; this interest, combined with extensive training in research, led her to the writing of biographies. In her three books—*The Lives and Times of Peter Cooper, Restless Spirit: The Life of Edna St. Vincent Millay,* and *Clarence Darrow*—her main purpose was to select representative individuals and present them against the background of their times.

Mrs. Gurko was graduated from the University of Wisconsin where she majored in history and anthropology. It was there that she met and married her husband, Leo Gurko, who is now a professor of English at Hunter College. After graduating, Mrs. Gurko worked for several magazines and for a publishing house specializing in Americana; she helped prepare a historical survey of the family for an educational organization; and she worked with an archaeological foundation devoted to the culture of the Middle East. While her two children were growing up, she wrote many magazine articles.

Mrs. Gurko was born in Union City, New Jersey, and grew up in Weehawken. She and her husband now live in New York City in an apartment overlooking the Hudson River.